John Dobson
Newcastle Architect
1787-1865

John Dobson
Newcastle Architect
1787-1865

by
Tom Faulkner
and
Andrew Greg

Published to celebrate the bicentenary of the architect's birth
in conjunction with an exhibition held at the Laing Art Gallery, Newcastle upon Tyne,
10th October — 29th November 1987.

Sponsored by Christie's
— Fine Art Auctioneers Since 1766 —
and by Tyne Tees Television
with additional assistance from
The City of Newcastle upon Tyne.

TYNE TEES

TYNE AND WEAR MUSEUMS SERVICE

ISBN 0 905974 31 X

© 1987 Tyne and Wear Museums Service

Printed by Hindson Print, Newcastle upon Tyne

Photographic Acknowledgements

Authors (6, 17, 20, 46, 63, 65, 75, 81)
Bildarchiv Foto Marburg (82)
Cheshire Libraries and Museums, Warrington Library
    (104)
Country Life (26, 31)
Duke of Northumberland (4)
Durham County Record Office (I)
Gateshead M.B.C. Libraries and Arts Department (71)
Lord Hastings (15)
R.N. McKellar and Partners (34)
National Monuments Record (7, 9, 24, 25, 36, 52, 53, 59,
    100)
National Trust (78)
Newcastle Central Library (18, 35, 44, 50, 51, 52, 55,
    66, 67, 73, 76, 77, 79, 84, 93, 96)
Newcastle University (57)
Major Philip Riddell (13, 14)
South Shields Library (72)
Tyne and Wear Archives (19, 101)
Tyne and Wear Museums Service (II, III, IV, V, VI, front
    cover, title page, 1, 2, 3, 5, 10, 16, 22, 30, 33, 37, 43, 47,
    48, 54, 62, 67, 68, 69, 74, 83, 86, 90, 91, 92, 97, 102,
    103, 105)
Rik Walton (8, 11, 12, 21, 23, 27, 28, 29, 38, 40, 41, 42,
    45, 49, 52, 56, 58, 61, 64, 70, 80, 85, 88, 89)
Whitby Literary and Philosophical Society (98)

Contents

Authors' Acknowledgements

This book and its accompanying exhibition would have been impossible without the help of many individuals and institutions.

Foremost have been the owners of Dobson's buildings who have answered letters, and allowed us to visit and photograph them. This book should be dedicated to those who have both the pleasure and problems of living with Dobson's architecture.

His Honour Judge Wilkes, the doyen of Dobson studies, has given us his continuous support and encouragement for which we are immensely grateful. Our research was given a firm foundation by the labours of Sandy Chamberlain whose invaluable extraction of local newspaper references is deposited in Newcastle Central Library. Further basic research was undertaken on our behalf by Sam Charlesworth, Kate Duncan and Mrs. Stella Mason. Dr. Lynn Pearson contributed to our discussion of Dobson's country house planning. Peter Meadows, who is researching Dobson's Durham contemporary Ignatius Bonomi, provided us with useful Durham newspaper references; Denis Perriam was of enormous help with Dobson's work in Cumbria and Graham Potts contributed to our knowledge of his Sunderland activities. Angus Fowler uncovered the details of Dobson's German castle commission, Peter Willis drew our attention to the beautiful Seaton Delaval album and David Rogers was extremely helpful with regard to the abortive Warrington Museum and Library proposal.

For the production of the book and the exhibition our first thanks must go to Christie's and Tyne Tees Television for their generous sponsorship. Location and studio photography was by Rik Walton of the Educational Development Service, Newcastle Polytechnic, Les Golding of Tyne and Wear Museums Service and Dennis Fitton of Newcastle City Engineers Department. The book was designed under the shadow of our inability to meet deadlines, though with unfailing good humour, by Vicki Taylor of Newcastle City Graphics Department.

Tom Faulkner
Andrew Greg

ABBREVIATIONS

AA	*Archaeologia Aeliana*
CL	*Country Life*
Collard and Ross	W. Collard and M. Ross, *Architectural and Picturesque Views in Newcastle upon Tyne*, 1841
DCRO	Durham County Record Office
Dobson	M.J. Dobson, *A Memoir of John Dobson*, 1885
Fordyce	W. Fordyce, *The History and Antiquities of ...Durham*, 1857
HMBCE	Historic Monuments and Buildings Commission for England
Hodgson	*History of Northumberland*, 1820-58
Hodgson 1832	*History of Morpeth*, 1832
ICBS	Incorporated Church Building Society
Latimer	John Latiner, *Local Records* 1857
Mackenzie 1811	E. Mackenzie, *Historical and Descriptive View of the County of Northumberland*, 1811
Mackenzie 1827	E. Mackenzie, *Descriptive and Historical Account ...of Newcastle upon Tyne*, 1827
Mackenzie and Ross	E. Mackenzie and M. Ross, *Historical, Topographical and Descriptive View of ... Durham*, 1834
Manders	F. Manders, *A History of Gateshead*, 1973
NA	*Newcastle Advertiser*
NC	*Newcastle Courant*
NCh	*Newcastle Chronicle*
NCC	Newcastle Central Library
NCRO	Northumberland County Record Office
NDJ	*Newcastle Daily Journal*
NJ	*Newcastle Journal*
Oliver	T. Oliver, *A New Picture of Newcastle upon Tyne*, 1831
Proc. Soc. Ant.	*Proceedings of the Society of Antiquaries of Newcastle upon Tyne*
RIBA	Royal Institute of British Architects
Sykes	J. Sykes, *Local Records*, 1866
TWA	Tyne and Wear Archives
Wilkes	Lyall Wilkes, *John Dobson, Architect and Landscape Gardner*, 1980
Wilkes and Dodds	Lyall Wilkes and Gordon Dodds, *Tyneside Classical*, 1964

Foreword

1987 is the bicentenary of the birth of John Dobson, but Tyne and Wear Museums Service needs no excuse to celebrate the life and work of a man who contributed more than any other to the architecture of the North East, and Tyneside in particular.

Born and bred in North Shields, educated and trained in Newcastle and London, Dobson brought to the region London's most fashionable ideas together with a Geordie's down-to-earth practicality. Immensely versatile in the range and styles of his buildings, he designed fine houses for the local gentry, noble crescents and squares for the middle classes, hotels and railway stations for travellers, and churches, schools, hospitals, baths and prisons for everyone.

Dobson is a figure of great importance, of whom all of us who live and work in the North East can justifiably feel proud.

This carefully researched book and its accompanying exhibition are the work of Tom Faulkner, Senior Lecturer in the History of Art and Design at Newcastle Polytechnic, and Andrew Greg of Tyne and Wear Museums Service. This association between the academic and the museum worlds has been a fruitful one in the past. We are sure that it will continue in the future to enlighten and entertain our public through similarly attractive and informative exhibitions and publications.

We would like to express here our deep thanks to our two joint sponsors, Christie's and Tyne Tees Television, who have through their generosity enabled the book and the exhibition to be produced to a very high standard. The Director of Architecture, Design and Environment, British Railways Board, has generously financed additional supporting publications and financial assistance has also been made available by the City of Newcastle upon Tyne. The partnership, exemplified here, between Local Authorities and business will become increasingly important in coming years and is now recognised as one in which the mutual benefits are readily realisable.

We are confident that this book will ensure that Dobson's work and the architectural environment he helped to create will reach a wide audience and be appreciated all the more in the future. This is especially important at a time when the tourist potential of the region's towns and cities is beginning to be recognised and exploited.

Councillor Barney Rice
Chairman, Tyne and Wear Museums Joint Committee

John Thompson
Director, Tyne and Wear Museums Service

I *The Early Years 1787-1810*

By the end of the 18th century North Shields had grown from a decaying and impoverished fishing village into a prosperous and fashionable port. Its quays sent coal from the newly developed coalfields of Northumberland down to London and its roperies and anchor foundries supplied the local shipyards. High on the banks of the Tyne smart Georgian terraces and squares had been built for the shipowners, mariners and manufacturers of the area. A few miles inland the villages of Chirton and Preston lay as yet relatively untouched by industry and commerce; Chirton, with a population of under 1000 was dominated by the mansion houses of the Collingwoods and the Lawsons. However, a wagonway just west of Chirton crossed the muddy Newcastle turnpike and carried coal from Shiremoor and Murton down to the staithes at Whitehill Point and smoke from the steam engine at nearby Percy Main colliery would often have drifted over the village.

John Dobson was born at his parents' home in Chirton on 9th December 1787[1]. His father, John Dobson Senr., a native of Stamfordham, in addition to owning a public house, was in business on a large scale as a market gardener. 'The beautiful and extensive fruit gardens of Mr. Dobson', Mackenzie wrote, 'render Chirton a place of fashionable resort during the summer months. They are tastefully laid out with pleasant walks and convenient seats and arbours for the accommodation of parties of pleasure. Mr. D. has other gardens for the growth of vegetables, of which great quantities are consumed by the town and shipping of Shields'[2]. He was also occasionally employed to lay out ornamental pleasure grounds, a talent he was to pass on to his son.

In this pleasant and workmanlike environment of ornamental yet productive gardens, country villages and early signs of the industrial revolution, whose wealth was to provide so much of his future patronage, Dobson spent his childhood. He later remembered the Tyne of his youth as being 'little short of Paradise', covered in trees and flowering shrubs down to the water's edge, from Newcastle to Shields. Within his lifetime it was to be transformed from rural bliss to a hive of industrial activity. His father evidently intended him to follow in the gardening profession and gave him instruction to that end. He also gained some experience on the Earl of Strathmore's estate at Gibside in County Durham. The young boy's artistic talent soon showed itself however and, with the encouragement of the local schoolmaster and eventually his father, he became well known locally for his botanical drawings. This led to occasional employment, while still in his early teens as draughtsman to a damask and linen weaver at nearby Preston, Mr. J. McGlashan, and to a grazier and butcher at North Shields, Mr. Ratcliffe.

1. John Dobson's bookplate, c.1820? (Laing Art Gallery, Newcastle upon Tyne)

2. The Mouth of the Tyne, c.1800. From an aquatint by W.H. Timms after R. Parker (Laing Art Gallery, Newcastle upon Tyne)

Sometime in the early 1800s Dobson went to Newcastle to study under Boniface Muss, who taught perspective and landscape painting, fencing and Italian, several of the necessary elements in the education of young gentlemen and women. There he was a fellow pupil of his exact contemporary, John Martin (1787-1854), who was later to achieve great fame as a painter of dramatic literary and historic subjects, often incorporating immense architectural perspectives. Martin, like Muss, left Newcastle in 1805 to pursue a career as a china painter in London.

The Newcastle of 1800 was a town still largely confined within its medieval walls. However, in the previous two decades it had struggled to accommodate its narrow, steep thoroughfares to the demands of a burgeoning commercial and industrial economy. Dean Street and Mosley Street were built in 1787 to improve the only road route from the Tyne Bridge northwards. The walls and gates along the Quayside were being demolished; the Tyne Bridge itself was widened in 1801. New public buildings, such as the Assembly Rooms, All Saints' Church and the Guildhall and Exchange introduced a previously unknown classical purity to the provincial architecture of the town and were evidence of the growing prosperity and sophistication of its inhabitants. The town itself was expanding northwards, above and beyond the overcrowded Chares, tenements and warehouses of the Close, the Quayside and Sandgate. Elegant new residential streets and squares had arisen beyond the town walls. Westgate Hill and Saville Row lay newly built among open fields.

Down on the river an ever-widening range of industry was spread along both banks. Staithes unloaded coal wagons from the Tyneside pits for eventual consumption in London and abroad. Steam engines were allowing deeper and more productive pits to be sunk. Iron, glass, paper and soap works, roperies, shipyards and potteries were rapidly expanding. In addition, the Tyne served as a port for the whole North East of England, exporting lead, grain and grindstone as well as local manufactures. Much of the investment for all these new enterprises came from local landowners who had also been involved in the traditional rural industries not only of agriculture, but also of textiles, lime-burning and lead-mining. The interrelation of many of these industries made the Tyne a centre of the country's fledgeling chemical industry, and the financial requirements of such large scale and complex investments had given rise to some of Britain's earliest provincial banks.

4

3

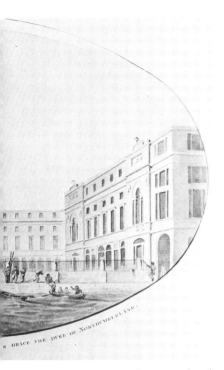

3. David Stephenson: All Saints' Church, Newcastle upon Tyne 1786—96. From an aquatint by Robert Pollard after Robert Hardy, 1799 (Laing Art Gallery, Newcastle upon Tyne)

4. David Stephenson: Intended New Market Place and Quay, North Shields. From a watercolour by Dobson, 1810 (The Duke of Northumberland)

Carried along by this flourishing industrial environment were the necessary trades and professions that created the increasing middle class in Newcastle and hence the continuing demand for good quality, sophisticated urban housing already referred to. The industrialists and landowners themselves had houses in the country. Some were medieval castles, most of them decayed and severely uncomfortable; others were the result of new 18th century wealth from coal and the shiping trade. All were ripe for further improvement and restoration in the 19th century.

Soon after beginning to study with Muss, Dobson expanded his interests to encompass a more practical study of architecture by being instructed in mechanical and architectural drawing by Mr. Hall of Stamfordham, bridge surveyor for Northumberland. He further confirmed his commitment to the architectural profession sometime around 1804 by entering into an apprenticeship with David Stephenson, then Newcastle's and the North East's leading architect. Stephenson had been born in 1757 and had made his name with his impressive design for All Saints' Church in Newcastle, built between 1786 and 1796. The building typifies Stephenson's brand of delicate neoclassicism, combining an inventive oval plan with a finely detailed spire, all decorated with the characteristic urns, swags and fluted columns of the late 18th century. He was architect to Newcastle Corporation from 1788 and in 1794 designed the new north front of the Guildhall and Exchange with William Newton, architect of St. Anne's Church and the Assembly Rooms. At the time of Dobson's apprenticeship, Stephenson was about to be appointed architect to the Duke of Northumberland, for whom his most important design was to be the uncompleted proposal for a new Market Place and Quay at North Shields.

By 1800 architectural apprenticeships had become the usual mode of formal architectural training, usually lasting for five or six years from the age of 16. The years of Dobson's late teens were thus spent in Stephenson's office assisting him in his work and thereby learning all the skills necessary to the work of the professional architect: dealing with clients and contractors, estimating and surveying, drawing up designs and working drawings and supervising contractors' work. Stephenson's practice does not seem to have been very large however; recorded works are few. Those after 1800 are almost all connected with his work for the Duke of Northumberland. The most important of these, the North Shields Market Place, would have been planned and begun during the time of Dobson's apprenticeship. This was one of the most ambitious pieces of neoclassical public architecture in the North of England and has much in common with urban designs by Robert Adam, particularly those for the Adelphi (1768-72) and Fitzroy Square (1790) in London, and for the planning of Edinburgh in the 1780s. As a northern architect, Stephenson would have had ample opportunity to witness the dramatic transformation of Edinburgh as the building work progressed slowly through the 1790s and early 1800s. Of particular relevance in this context are the designs for Edinburgh University, Charlotte Square and the South Bridge development.

Dobson's possible contribution to Stephenson's design is impossible to determine and in fact largely irrelevant as his earliest classical designs adopted wholeheartedly the new Greek Revival style and he never worked in Stephenson's and Adam's neoclassical style. By 1810, when Dobson made the attractive oval perspective view of the intended Market Place appended to a large plan of North Shields, Stephenson's design was stylistically quite outdated and Dobson had won his first important commission, for the Royal Jubilee School in Newcastle, in a characteristically robust Greek Revival style.

Architectural apprentices would, if they could afford it, travel abroad at the end of their apprenticeships, through Europe to Rome and Greece, to study the monuments of classical antiquity and of the Italian Renaissance. Dobson, of lesser means, travelled to London after completing his clerkship with Stephenson in 1809. Somewhat curiously, in view of his evident dedication to architecture, he spent some time studying watercolour painting with the successful watercolourist and fashionable teacher, John Varley. The suggestions by other authors that Varley did not want pupils are unfounded; he was and is well known as an influential teacher, both in person and through his publications. Varley had toured the North East of England in 1808 sketching the castles and other picturesque sites of the region and teaching watercolour painting to the families of the Northumberland gentry. It is possible that Dobson first met him on this occasion. Certainly within a year or two Dobson was one of his pupils. A watercolour of Lindisfarne of c.1810-11 in the Victoria and Albert Museum is inscribed on the back 'Mr. Dobson', identifying it as being a drawing he was required to copy. The relationship clearly matured into friendship.

6

Dobson probably sought out Varley in order to acquire the facility in watercolour necessary to produce the newly fashionable colour perspectives with which architects were beginning to present their designs to clients. However, as we shall see, Dobson was eventually to rely almost exclusively on John Wilson Carmichael to work up his perspective drawings into dramatic and effective watercolours. A large and conventional landscape watercolour supposedly made during Dobson's time with Varley is in the Laing Art Gallery; it does bear some of the characteristics of the master's style. More obvious in the surviving early architectural drawings by Dobson is a distinctly 18th century flavour, in the elongated figures in the large perspective of the Royal Jubilee School, or the Bewick-like vignettes in the album of William Clark's Estates, for example. The perspective of St. Thomas's Church of c.1827 is the first surviving drawing of the partnership of Dobson and Carmichael, and in this the talent of an accomplished landscape watercolourist is more evident.

Other well known artists have been mentioned as being friends of Dobson from this time, Turner, Mulready and Benjamin West, for example, and there is some evidence to support this. Mulready, Linnell and W.H. Hunt all studied under Varley and were closely associated around 1810, and Dobson would very probably have known them; West is quoted by Dobson in his 1859 Presidential Address to the Northern Architectural Association[3]. One important figure we can be surer of his knowing was the architect Robert Smirke, then a rising star on the architectural scene. His recently completed Covent Garden Theatre was a pioneering example of the newly fashionable Greek Revival. Smirke's younger brother, Sydney, also an architect, was to marry Dobson's eldest daughter in 1840.

The opportunity to study the current architectural scene in London was more important to Dobson's development as an architect than Varley's watercolour instruction. The first decade of the 19th century was a highly important one in the history of architectural design. In 1803, Elgin's marbles, removed from the finest Greek temple, the Parthenon in Athens, arrived in London. There they excited controversy between enthusiastic artists and sceptical connoisseurs, but finally convinced architects of the supreme virtues of Greek art. They were on public exhibition in London from 1807. The leaders of the Greek Revival in architecture, William Wilkins and Robert Smirke, were both travelling in Greece in that decade; Wilkins in 1801, Smirke in 1803. The discoveries, excavations, surveys and publications of those and other architects and collectors confirmed the importance of Stuart and Revett's pioneering publication of *The Antiquities of Athens* (1762-1795) and from then on Greek mania pervaded not only architecture but novels, poetry, fashion, furniture and all aspects of design. The first major examples of the Greek Revival in English architecture were built in this decade, Wilkins' Grange Park, 1804-9, and Downing College, from 1807, Smirke's Covent Garden Theatre, 1808-9, and John Soane's Bank of England interiors were begun. Before 1800 the Greek Revival was 'the plaything of a few private patrons', after 1810 it became the established style of public buildings throughout the country.

7

6. Sir Charles Monck: Belsay Hall, Northumberland, from 1807

7. A Greek Doric Temple from an engraving after William Wilkins, 1806 (Private collection)

8. John Stokoe: The Moot Hall, Newcastle upon Tyne, 1810—11

8

The powerful austerity of the style seems particularly well suited to Scotland, where it continued with undimmed vigour into the 1850s, and to the North of England. Thomas Harrison's Chester Castle of 1785-1820 pioneered the style for public buildings; at Belsay in Northumberland, Sir Charles Monck was his own architect for 'the finest Greek Revival mansion in the country', and in Newcastle John Stokoe's Moot Hall of 1810 was the best of the provincial responses to Smirke's Covent Garden.

Dobson's involvement in the design of Belsay Hall, being built from 1807, has often been quoted but never been proved; there is little more than circumstantial evidence. But there is no doubt that on his return to Newcastle in 1810 he would have found the existence of Belsay and the Moot Hall powerful encouragement to promote Greek Revival architecture of the purest and highest quality in the North East of England.

When Dobson set up practice on Tyneside, initially basing himself in Chirton, his birthplace, he and his friend Ignatius Bonomi were, according to his own words, 'the only professional architects in the Counties of Northumberland and Durham'. Dobson was careful to maintain the distinctions of status and financial situation between the profession of architect and the trade and business of the builder. He had entered the architectural profession at the very time that it was struggling to create and define its identity. In 1834, with the creation of the Institute of British Architects, the process was complete, but in 1810 builder-architects, like John Stokoe, who was the designer *and* builder of the Moot Hall, were more typical. Dobson made a deliberate decision on leaving Stephenson's office, and with the latter's counsel and advice, to set up in Newcastle as a professional architect, in the modern sense.

However, even in London, the architectural profession was already overcrowded and the provinces were as yet unused to this new breed of professional. Dobson acknowledged that in the first few years of his career there was little demand for his services, but it seems that his first success, and a major coup for a young architect, may have been obtained before he had even returned to settle in the North East.

Notes

1 The principal sources for Dobson's early life are Fordyce, 1857, III, p.765 and M. J. Dobson.

2 Mackenzie 1811, II, p.560.

3 Reprinted in Wilkes, pp.99—110.

10

II *The Making of an Architect 1810-1823*

The Royal Jubilee School in City Road, Newcastle, was built to designs by Dobson which were approved by the subscribers on 23rd March 1810. The advertisement requesting builders' estimates, however, stated that these were to be received by John Stokoe in his office at The Manors, rather than by Dobson. Dobson's authorship is unquestionable[1]; presumably his absence in London forced him to entrust the supervision of the School to the builder-architect John Stokoe. The school was built to honour George III's Jubilee wish that 'every poor child in the Kingdom be able to read the Bible' and consisted of a stark rectangle in pure Greek temple form. The Doric portico is taken straight from Robert Smirke's recently completed pioneering Covent Garden Theatre, but returned to its 'correct' position at the gable-end of a roof. It is also more correct than John Stokoe's contemporary north entrance to the Moot Hall where the columns are unevenly spaced. However, in a strange foreshadowing of the incomplete execution of Newcastle's Central Station at the climax of Dobson's career, this school, his first building, was also built without its portico.

On his return to the North East and for the first two years of his professional practice, Dobson was based at Chirton, presumably in his parents' house. His work in these early years was split between North Shields and Newcastle; local contacts in and around North Shields enabled him to build up a solid base of domestic, institutional and industrial work there.

In view of the relative sophistication of this early design, it is somewhat surprising to find a year later in 1811 the rather crude Greek Revival Meeting House for the Scotch Presbyterians in Howard Street, North Shields. This is another severe neoclassical building, its three bay facade with Doric pilasters having some resemblance to that of the Royal Jubilee School as built. However, the Greek temple effect, with steps leading up to the front in both designs, is less pronounced in the case of the Meeting House since it has no pediment, its entablature being surmounted by a tall attic storey. The mouldings above the windows on the ground floor are supported by brackets embellished with a curious motif of animal skulls. This was followed in 1812 by a

9. Dobson's house, New Bridge Street, Newcastle upon Tyne, 1823

10. Presbyterian Church, Howard Street, North Shields, 1811

11. The Royal Jubilee School, Newcastle upon Tyne, 1810. From a watercolour by Dobson (Laing Art Gallery, Newcastle upon Tyne)

11

Methodist Chapel in Newcastle, sited opposite the Royal Jubilee School on New Road. It was an extremely plain classical building of two storeys with a facade of five bays, the middle three slightly recessed, and steps leading to entrance doors, flanking three round arched windows, at each end of the street front.

Dobson's first major work for the local Anglicans took place between 1818 and 1820, when he carried out extensive alterations to Gosforth Parish Church, a handsome but undersized structure of 1799. He added a north and south aisle with galleries, connecting with a gallery already present at the west[2]. Dobson worked in a manner compatible with the simple classicism of the existing church, and indeed enhanced it by providing Tuscan columns supporting elegant shallow arches to divide the aisles from the nave. He did not extend the length of the church, however, and his virtually cruciform plan of 1818 was substantially enlarged in 1884, and again in 1913 when the nave was almost doubled in length. These extensions are in accordance with the style of Dobson's original work, at the time of which he also built at the edge of the churchyard a little rustic cottage for the sexton, only recently demolished, in a rudimentary Tudor mode.

Dobson had made further inroads into Newcastle by selling building sites in Jesmond for Thomas Burdon as early as February 1811, and again in March at Barras Bridge, perhaps for the same patron. Thomas Burdon was an important figure in Newcastle at the time. He had been elected Mayor in 1810 and was to be knighted in 1816 as a reward for putting down the 1815 sailors' strike. To work for Burdon, even in such a humble capacity, would undoubtedly have been an extremely valuable introduction into the Northumberland and Newcastle oligarchy of squires, merchants and landowners. Dobson was to work for Burdon again in 1814 selling building land, and won an important architectural commission from him in 1817 for the design of West Jesmond House (see below).

With this and the other useful contacts he had made through the Royal Jubilee School, Dobson felt able to move to Newcastle in the early summer of 1812, to an office in Pilgrim Street. In the three years, 1810-12, only three buildings by Dobson are recorded; immediately after his move to Newcastle work came considerably faster and expanded to include his first houses and his first work in County Durham.

Field House in Gateshead, built in 1813 for George Barras was Dobson's first house design. Unfortunately, despite surviving until the 1930s, the only record of its appearance is a poor pen and ink drawing which tells us that it was plain, classical and with a hipped roof undisguised by a parapet[3]. We have more information about a major remodelling undertaken in the same year for Henry Riddell at Cheeseburn Grange in Northumberland. The survival of both the house and of Dobson's original album of designs gives us the opportunity to look in detail at several aspects of Dobson's work at this time[4].

Cheeseburn was a seventeenth century farm house, embellished in the eighteenth century with a baroque doorcase in the centre of the south front and, according to Dobson's drawing of the house before he began work on it, Tudor-style drip mouldings around the windows. Dobson took the opportunity to extend the Tudor treatment to the whole house. He moved the entrance to the side, raised a short tower over it, and sheltered it with plantations, a feature of many of his future house designs. He embellished the skyline with turrets and small hexagonal towers, crowned with castellations at the corners, and raised a high parapet, pierced with gothic openings, to hide the old roof. Castellated offices completed the ensemble.

Dobson's proposals are important for also including major alterations to the surrounding parkland. He built a ha-ha to blend yet separate the house and its park, suggested a whole new scheme of replanting, designed a new gateway and lodge and replanned the driveway to enable the visitor on his approach to the house to fully appreciate the siting of the house in its landscape. The lodge is a deliberately primitive cottage, in the by then well-established tradition of cottage architecture, set deep in trees, with a thatched roof and diamond-paned windows. These landscaping elements follow the example of Humphrey Repton who restructured the rather formless approach to landscape gardening of Capability Brown. Repton's most important contributions were the revival of formal elements, terraces, borders, paths and lawns, in the immediate vicinity of a house (which Dobson was to make a trademark of his houses within a few years); the emphasis on the situation of a house within a landscape (as seen in this plan for Cheeseburn); and a thorough botanical knowledge of trees and shrubs (which Dobson with his horticultural background would have shared). Dobson, it is clear, was in a good position to benefit from the popular and practical books through which Repton publicised his theories.

12. St. Nicholas's, Gosforth, 1818—20

13. Cheeseburn Grange, Northumberland, 1813. Dobson's proposed entrance front (Major Philip Riddell)

14. Cheeseburn Grange, Northumberland, 1813, the park. Dobson's proposed improvements (Major Philip Riddell)

12

WEST ELEVATION

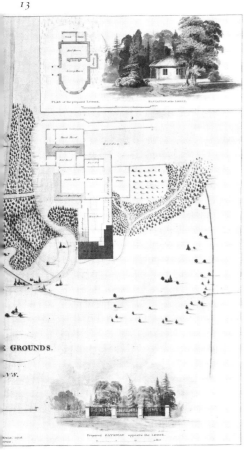

13

Dobson's interest in landscape gardening, particularly evident in these early years, is also illustrated by his work at Bolam in Northumberland for the Hon. W.H. Beresford in 1816. There he laid out an artificial lake, 'necessary islands' and adjoining plantations, so that the estate might be both attractive and productive. Thirty years later he commented knowledgeably on the lack of attention that the estate had subsequently received[5].

At Cheeseburn, Dobson was engaged in the fashionable updating of a plain house; in two other fortunately well documented commissions of the following years we can study other aspects of his increasingly popular role as an improver of older houses.

Two beautiful drawings made by Dobson in 1814 for the Earl of Strathmore[6] concerned alterations to Gibside in County Durham, an early seventeenth century house which had already been much enlarged in 1805. Here the Earl had inherited one of the finest eighteenth century landscape gardens in the North of England and he continued his predecessors' interest in horticulture and gardening by commissioning Dobson to design a large conservatory which was to be added to the west end of the house. This charming building, of cast iron and glass, fed by rainwater and heated by hot air from an adjacent furnace, combined these most practical considerations with an expression of the Regency period's delight in being able to walk directly from the house into a conservatory full of luxuriant and exotic plants. Again, Dobson's background in gardening was to be particularly useful in a period which valued highly the interrelation of architecture and nature. It is a theme we shall have cause to return to later.

At Seaton Delaval in Northumberland, the most important eighteenth century country house in the North East, Dobson proposed to Sir Jacob Henry Astley alterations and additions intended to improve the appearance of the house. The design of Vanbrugh's superb, but impractical, house of 1718-28 had been seriously marred in the latter part of the century by the addition of a large wing, extending the south elevation seven bays to the east. The wing ended with a forward breaking bay and a large east-facing bay window. Dobson proposed, in an elaborately conceived album of drawings[7] dating from 1814-17, to rebuild the east end of the wing so as to conform closely, perhaps even pedantically, with Vanbrugh's architectural detailing, with octagonal corner towers repeating exactly the form of those on the central block. More grandiosely, Dobson also proposed the building of a matching west wing which would have created an enormous south front of 23 bays. However, these proposals did not survive the death of Sir Jacob Astley in 1817. He may have intended to carry them out as they appear in contemporary engravings and paintings of the house, but his successor seemed little interested in building. When the main block of the house was gutted by fire in 1822, Dobson may also have been consulted concerning its restoration (in 1838 he exhibited a water colour of its restored state), but in the event it was not until 1860, after a further change of ownership, that Dobson eventually reroofed the block and enabled what remained of the house's architectural glories to survive to the present day.

At Gibside and Seaton Delaval, Dobson was dealing with long-established aristocratic families. The elaborateness of presentation of both sets of designs and the fact that neither was carried out suggest the possibility that they were perhaps unsolicited; that Dobson made them more to bring his talents and ambition to the notice of potentially important and influential patrons than in the hope of their resulting in immediate work. Judging by the work attributed to him in the next few years this presumption may have paid off. Several other important eighteenth century country houses in Northumberland and Durham have evidence or suggestions of his work, most commonly in improving their comfort.

In his 1859 Address to the Northern Architectural Association[8], Dobson stressed how the formal planning of eighteenth century houses encouraged the continual cold draughts which plagued inhabitants and visitors. A north or south entrance, always overlooking an open view, led directly into the staircase hall and thence into the principal corridors and rooms. As we have seen, Dobson's solution at Cheeseburn, as in his own later houses, was to place the entrance in a sheltered facade at the side; in his alterations to James Paine's Axwell Park in County Durham, Belford Hall, Bywell Hall and Gosforth Park in Northumberland, the work included making the rear, the north and more sheltered, entrance the principal one. At Belford, for example, an Ionic colonnade and a new entrance hall fill in part of Paine's rear courtyard. There he was working for a patron, William Clark, for whom he had previously made a charming series of estate plans including land at Cullercoats, Little Benton, Monkseaton and New Whitley around 1812-13[9].

The classical houses of the North East may have been relatively uncomfortable, but the older country seats were mostly in a far worse state. Not only were they inconvenient and decayed to such a degree that few were habitable at all, but architecturally they were often mongrel affairs consisting of work of several different periods. Most distressingly, to the increasing number of patrons and architects who were sensitive to the architecture of the Gothic and Elizabethan periods, many had been 'improved' in the eighteenth century by the introduction of large rectangluar sash windows into their facades. Such was the case at Chipchase Castle where both the fourteenth century tower and the adjoining Jacobean house of 1621 received a complete set of regular sash windows in 1784. Dobson's work on the house in 1819 seems to have involved the restoration of Jacobean-style fenestration to the bay windows. Characteristic of this period also is that the patron of this work was not from a family of ancient Northumbrian lineage, but Colonel John Reed, a partner in the Newcastle bank Blake, Reed and Co. In 1842 the failure of the bank caused him to sell the house, however.

Among the few other pre-eighteenth century houses with which Dobson was involved in this period was Rock Hall in Northumberland. Here Dobson made significant additions as well as generally 'tidying up' the picturesque sixteenth and seventeenth century house. Much of it is now ruinous, but the most obvious, indeed discordant, evidence of Dobson's work of 1819 is the pair of broad octagonal towers symmetrically placed on the south side. These attempted to provide modern living accommodation for the house while also contributing, unsuccessfully, to the picturesque informality of the whole composition. The rather heavy, unsubtle and plain additions show, like Cheeseburn, how little Dobson, or most architects of his generation, had learnt of the true spirit or character of Gothic architecture.

The eighteenth century is rightly seen as above all a period of classical architecture. It was an age deeply sympathetic to the rational and functional aspects of classical architecture and to its association with the intellectual traditions of the well ordered and democratic societies of Greece and Rome. But a thread of Gothic survived and ran through the century, principally as a superficial decorative style, only appropriate for ornamental buildings in parks, such as Daniel Garrett's Banqueting House at Gibside of 1751, or for the whimsical enjoyment of an amateur such as Horace Walpole at Strawberry Hill. Towards the end of the century, the irregularity and visual potential of the Gothic style was given sanction by theories of the Picturesque which stressed the

15

16

ctive View of the South Front of the HOUSE showing the proposed Addition & Alteration

15. Seaton Delaval, Northumberland, c.1814—17. Dobson's proposed additions (Lord Hastings)

16. Seaton Delaval, Northumberland. Watercolour by Dobson, 1818 (Laing Art Gallery, Newcastle upon Tyne)

17. Rock Hall, Northumberland, 1819. Dobson's additions to the south side

visual qualities of variety, texture and informality. Thus, Gothic, 'Tudor-Gothic' and castellated styles could and did flourish side by side with classically derived architecture. Among the most important proponents of these styles in the early 19th century was Robert Smirke who, as well as being at the forefront of the Greek Revival, was highly influential for his dramatic compositions in the castle style. William Wilkins too, famous for the purity of his Greek detailing, designed in the Gothic style

18

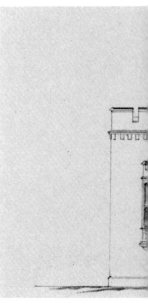

19

where appropriate. Smirke's first architectural success, Lowther Castle in Cumberland, building from 1806-11, is in the castellated Gothic style and as a highly important northern example must have been familiar to Dobson. Smirke's castle style, like Robert Adam's, is characterised by a strict symmetry in which every tower and pointed window is echoed, and the whole composition builds up to the central climax of a large square tower. Another stimulating local example of domestic Gothic Revival architecture must have been the 'monster castle' of Ravensworth, a few miles south-west of Gateshead. Based on designs made by John Nash in 1807-8, Ravensworth evolved over the next forty years, long after Nash's death, under the direction of Lord Ravensworth's son, Thomas Henry Liddell. Before about 1822, however, building was continuing to Nash's designs. Though it was to finish up even larger, Nash's original plans show a house which would have been the largest Gothic house in the North of England. In contrast to Smirke's castellated houses at Lowther and Eastnor, Ravensworth was to be consciously asymmetric in the manner pioneered by the theorist of the Picturesque Richard Payne Knight at Downton in the 1770s and adopted by Nash as an essential element in non-classical architecture.

Thus, at the time Dobson was building up his professional practice, the two traditions of design, classical and Gothic, were well established and Dobson was well supplied with new and important examples. In addition to his travels in England and France, he had access to numerous, if superficial, books of Gothic designs from which to gain inspiration. Neither Rock Hall nor Cheeseburn Grange show the result of much benefit from these sources, but these were still for Dobson years of study, as he made clear in his 1859 Address.

Early designs for new Gothic houses, in which he was less restricted by existing fabric, were made for Sir Thomas Burdon at West Jesmond House (later Jesmond Towers) and for Thomas Emerson Headlam at Black Dene House (later Jesmond Dene House). Burdon, we have already met; Headlam was a leading local Whig politician, twice Mayor of Newcastle and strong supporter of Earl Grey's moves towards Reform, also an important local surgeon. Both these houses have complicated building histories, but both have become the most important survivors of the varied phases and manifestations of the nineteenth century Gothic Revival in Newcastle. Black Dene House, worked on by Dobson in 1822 and, for William Cruddas, in 1851, was added to by Richard Norman Shaw in the 1870s and 1880s and Dobson's work was completely rebuilt by F.W. Rich in 1896. Dobson's work at Jesmond Towers is still extant, but embedded in substantial, but conservative, additions by Thomas Oliver of 1869 and T.R. Spence of 1885. The appearance of the house before 1869 is fortunately recorded in Oliver's drawing of the house as it then existed, though this

20

18. John Nash and T. H. Liddell:
Ravensworth Castle, Durham, 1807 onwards

19. Thomas Oliver: West Jesmond House,
Newcastle upon Tyne in 1865. The south
front showing Dobson's work of 1823—7
(Tyne and Wear Archives)

20. West Jesmond House, Newcastle upon
Tyne. Reconstruction of Dobson's north
front of 1817

may include work by Burdon's son, Richard Burdon Sanderson, of 1833[10]. Two phases of building, corresponding presumably to Dobson's two periods of work there of 1817 and 1823-7, are clearly visible and distinct in style and orientation. The north side, with its wide, relatively plain windows and solid octagonal corner turrets, represents the earlier house, reflecting the solidity of the Smirke castle style, as well as Dobson's own work at Cheeseburn. This front, overlooking Jesmond Dene, originally had a high terrace hiding the basement and was only of three floors; the fourth was added by Oliver. The south side is Dobson's work of 1823-7, also symmetrical, but on a different axis to the north facade, and with corner towers and battlements elaborately decorated, the windows more richly traceried. Like his contemporary Lying-in Hospital, the details, though well observed, are a mixture of Decorated and Perpendicular elements.

Dobson's assured handling of the Greek Revival style, on the other hand, came early, as is obvious in the designs for the Royal Jubilee School. Within a few years of beginning work he had adopted and was promoting the style in his domestic work. None of these early houses, Gothic or classical, were large; they were what their contemporaries would have thought of as villas, houses for men of moderate means, or country retreats for the gentry of the towns.

The notion of the villa had been given architectural form in the mid 18th century by architects such as Robert Taylor and James Paine, and became the ideal vehicle of expression for the variety of picturesque styles prevalent at the end of the century. Despite its serious intellectual overtones, the Greek Revival was just one more decorative style available for the rural architect. Even by 1805 the Greek style was to the compiler of architectural pattern books no more important than the Gothic, Castle, and Roman, to which list Old English and Italian could be added by 1830. The Grecian villa in its landscaped parkland was as picturesque an object as the ruined church or rustic bridge. Nonetheless the Greek style did have serious meaning to the young gentleman returning from the Grand Tour, or any patron with artistic and intellectual interests. It tended to appeal to the mind while Gothic appealed to the heart. The Greek style also had the advantage, not to be underestimated, of economy. The flat expanses of wall, regular windows with uncomplicated mouldings, and lack of external ornament saved the work of expensive craftsmen.

Many of Dobson's earliest houses, the majority of which were probably Greek, have been lost, especially those around North Shields, but there are three excellent examples surviving to illustrate his mastery of the style. Prestwick Lodge in Northumberland of 1815 is very plain; Greek detail is confined externally to the pilasters of the porch, the entrance hall being divided with two sturdy Greek Doric columns. At the Villa Reale in Newcastle the exterior is enlivened with a Doric portico on the entrance front and a large bay on the garden front, a foreshadowing of the facade arrangements of his mature houses of the 1820s and 1830s. But the sources for this attractive and ultimately 'picturesque' variation of design on the three facades of a house lie in the villas of John Soane and James Wyatt in the 1790s.

21

The interiors of these houses are plain and conventional, decorated with the characteristic motifs of the Greek Revival though with the addition of some more provincial naturalistic floral plasterwork that suggests the use of craftsmen not yet familiar with the 'correct' ornamental vocabulary. At Newbrough Park in Northumberland, however, with which Dobson may have been associated around 1821, the plasterwork copies motifs from Thomas Hope's *Household Furniture and Interior Decoration* of 1807, an influential compendium of the most fashionable Greek decorative designs.

The most impressive house of Dobson's early years is however Doxford Hall, a beautifully crafted Greek design of 1817-18 with projecting Doric portico *in antis* and, a rather old fashioned feature, two string courses between ground and first floors. It is placed in one of Dobson's most spectacular situations, high on a terrace above a wood-shrouded lake, surely also laid out by Dobson. The entrance front is a close relative of the even more sophisticated facade of Linden Hall, designed in all probability by Sir Charles Monck in 1812. Doxford would appear to be the first of Dobson's houses which benefitted from the exceptional masonry skills which Monck bequeathed to Northumberland following the completion of Belsay Hall. Dobson had good reasons to acknowledge the influence of the masons employed at Belsay: 'Sir Charles Monck... made the masonry of his new house equal to any of the polished marble temples of that classic land; this at once introduced a style of masonry previously unknown... The masons employed at Belsay... branched off into different parts of England, and since that time a Northumbrian mason has been considered amongst the best that could be found in any part of the country'[11].

21. Villa Reale, Newcastle upon Tyne, 1817

22. Doxford Hall, Northumberland, 1817—18

22

The importance that Dobson gives in his later houses to the hall and staircase is not apparent in these early designs; even at Doxford, one of the largest houses of this period, the hall led into a transverse corridor, off which leads a narrow staircase. No rooms intercommunicated; all led off the long corridor (this arrangement was altered in the early 20th century). This situation is further evidence of the influence of Cresswell Hall on Dobson's country house planning in the 1820s (see below p.24).

The overwhelming majority of Dobson's early designs were concerned with domestic architecture and it is as a domestic architect that he was to make his greatest achievements in the forthcoming decades.

Notes

1 See Mackenzie, 1811, II, p.743 for example.
2 Drawings by Dobson are in NCRO (NRO 1875/A(50)).
3 Reproduced in a newspaper cutting in Gateshead Central Library illustrations collection.
4 Collection of Major Philip Riddell.
5 NCRO (ZMI B/13/12).
6 DCRO (D/St/X/46a & 81a).
7 Album at Seaton Delaval.
8 Wilkes, p.105.
9 NCL.
10 TWA (T186/3615).
11 Wilkes, p.108.

III Country Houses, Greek and Gothic 1821-1840

Dobson's maturity as a country house architect lies in the 1820s as far as classical houses are concerned and in the 1830s with regard to Tudor and Gothic houses. This distinction reflects a national change in attitude towards styles in domestic architecture. The prolific architectural writer J.C. Loudon felt by 1833 that the classical style was unsuitable for the English countryside and should be confined to the town. Pugin, increasingly influential from the 1830s, added a moral element, that classical styles were pagan and only for the proud and worldly. In the light of the distinctions between the two decades, it makes sense to divide a study of Dobson's country houses, the most widely known of his designs, into these two overlapping stylistic groups.

The successful formula of the small square Greek country villa was one that Dobson had adopted effortlessly in the 1810s, at Prestwick and Doxford for example, and at other houses now lost. Their simplicity, indeed severity, and their craftsmanship in stone and plaster were in the spirit of the greatest Greek Revival house of all, Belsay Hall in Northumberland. The first house of the 1820s in this tradition is South Hill House, in County Durham, built for the banker Thomas Fenwick in 1821, but now dominated by a greatly enlarged service wing and with the later alterations to the entrance and the additions of bay windows the simplicity of Dobson's design has been lost. The chief remaining feature is the overlarge parapet intended to hide the hipped roof behind. Georgian classical architects preferred where possible to create a clean geometric composition by excluding any lines which were not horizontals or verticals. But Dobson's parapet here, as at Mitford Hall, is out of proportion and indeed projects beyond the walls of the house to overhang them, an unhappy situation.

23. Longhirst Hall, Northumberland, 1824-5. Carved spandrel in the hall ceiling

24. Mitford Hall, Northumberland, 1823—8

In all other respects Mitford Hall[1], near Morpeth in Northumberland, achieves the crisp subtlety of Doxford Hall. It was designed in 1823 for Bertram Osbaldeston Mitford, but building was delayed, perhaps because of the impending marriage of Dobson's patron, until 1828-29. Like the Moncks at Belsay, the Mitfords decided to leave their decaying medieval house and build anew nearby. The site is a typically Dobsonian one, designed with the optimum view, looking south over water, in this case the River Wansbeck. Here for the first time we find the full expression of Dobson's great subtlety of surface articulation, and of varied fenestration on the three principal facades. The entrance front has a projecting Greek Doric portico *in antis* placed in front of the narrower and slightly recessed central bay. The south front is plain and regular, the east of a yet different rhythm with a wider recessed central section containing three closely spaced windows. From this facade a low wing leads to a conservatory. The horizontal emphases are delicate and restrained; a slightly projecting base, a thread-like string course carrying the line of the porch's cornice round beneath the first floor windows, and a thin deeply projecting cornice.

Mitford Hall was designed in the same year that Dobson designed his own house in New Bridge Street as part of the development around the west end of the New Bridge over Pandon Dene in Newcastle upon Tyne. It is the sole survivor. Originally of ashlar, it is now brightly painted, but still displays the crisp simplicity of Dobson's 1820s classicism. The facade is uncomplicated by an entrance, which was placed to the side. A long garden behind contained his collection of architectural fragments.

Picton Place, which contained the best of Dobson's urban villas, was destroyed by the gradual expansion of the nearby railway sidings; but one of the larger houses, later known as 'Dobson's Villa' survived as the terminus of the Newcastle and Blyth Railway and later as an employment exchange. It was a substantial house, three by four bays, with an Ionic portico *in antis* in a slightly recessed centre bay, as at Mitford, and shallow Doric pilasters topped by isolated brackets.

Mitford Hall and Dobson's own house were rapidly followed by the designs for Longhirst Hall (1824), Dobson's finest classical design, and thus, as Dobson was always a classicist at heart, his best building[2].

Longhirst is not a large house, but its refinement of detail in masonry construction and carving, in plasterwork and in architectural design is almost faultless. Its general plan follows Mitford and conforms to a common pattern which Dobson may have derived from the important but now lost mansion of Cresswell Hall in Northumberland. Cresswell was built to the designs of the London architect John Shaw under the supervision of John Green from 1820 to 1824. It was a large square house with masonry work of Northumbrian quality and many design features shared by Dobson's best houses.

The archetypal Dobson house plan of the period places the reception rooms, various combinations of drawing room, library and dining room, along the south and east sides of the main square block of the house. Within this L-shape a smaller L-shape contains an entrance hall, entered from the west, and a staircase. The remaining corner contains a study or business room, not entered directly from the hall. To the north is the service wing and off that, to the east, a conservatory at the end of a linking wing.

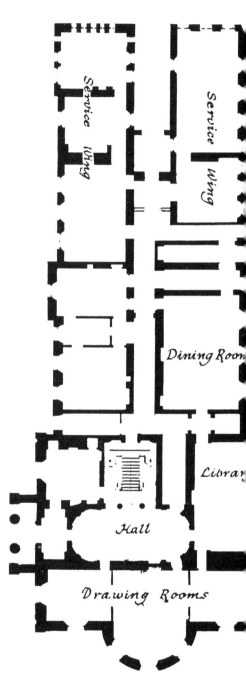

25. Picton Place, Newcastle upon Tyne, c.1825

26. Longhirst Hall, Northumberland, 1824—5. The ground-floor plan

27. Longhirst Hall, Northumberland, 1824—5

At Longhirst the plan is so compact that the dining room is squeezed out into the service wing, a departure from the ideal which has the advantage of placing the dining room nearer the kitchen.

Externally, the entrance front is dominated by the great portico of two giant Corinthian columns set *in antis* under the pediment. The use of a pediment is rare in Dobson's architecture, but here it allows him to omit his often unattractive parapet by making a virtue of the slope of the roof as echoed in the shape of the pediment.

In addition the powerful vertical emphasis of the portico balances the usual horizontal character of the Greek Revival style to create a perfectly satisfying composition. This is refined with immaculate masonry work, the most delicate and subtle cornice mouldings and pilaster strips at the corners, and superb stone carving in the Corinthians capitals over columns and pilasters. The south front features a large central bow, while the east front consists of a rank of five tall evenly spaced windows.

The quality of Longhirst's architecture is continued inside. The long oval hall, entered through a lobby, is an uncompromisingly severe space. Constructed of bare, unplastered masonry as solid as the exterior, it rises through two stories and is lit by three domes. On the ground floor decoration is kept to a minimum, a narrow honeysuckle frieze and brackets and two Ionic columns which frame the fine staircase. The ceiling of the first floor is made up of a series of coffered domes and a vault of austere character, but enlivened with excellent winged figures deeply carved in the pendentives. These are similar to those often used by John Soane, who was also very fond of shallow domes and segmental vaults.

The reception rooms contain some of the finest plasterwork to be found in Dobson's houses. It employs a wide variety of the usual neoclassical and Greek Revival motifs of a refinement and sophistication that suggests the use of the best pattern books, such as Thomas Hope's *Household Furniture and Interior Decoration* of 1807 and those by C.H. Tatham. Greek architectural ornament had been well publicised ever since Stuart and Revett's pioneering *Antiquities of Athens* (vol.1, 1762), but only came to full fruition in the decade of Mitford, Longhirst and

N

Billiard Room (post-Dobson)

Conservatory

26

28

29

Nunnykirk. The three drawing rooms at Longhirst were originally one long room with moveable partitions and have very fine ceilings. The dining room is exceptional for Dobson in having a pictorial frieze depicting a procession of classical figures and animals. Giant brackets, which indicate a shallow recess at the end of the room which would have held the sideboard, repeat exactly the carved oak brackets either side of the doorcase.

The flexibility of planning indicated in the drawing room is a sign of the informality of lifestyle enjoyed by early 19th century country house owners. So too are the large windows reaching almost from ceiling to floor, which encouraged the enjoyment of the view over garden and parkland and the blending of house and garden so typical of the period.

The owner of Longhirst Hall was William Lawson, from a farming family with long though relatively humble connections with Longhirst, and a relative of the Lawsons of Dobson's home village of Chirton. He had acquired his wealth through the exploitation of coal beneath his land. The patron of Dobson's next major classical work by contrast was a beneficiary of a more traditional mode of advancement within the landed gentry. William Orde inherited the Nunnykirk estate from his brother who had acquired it by marrying the heiress of William Ward, whose father had purchased it from the Greys of Chillingham, one of the oldest Northumberland landowners[3]. William Orde lived the life of a traditional country squire and became famous for his racehorses.

Dobson's work for Orde of 1825 involved the remodelling and enlargement of an earlier house, which is represented by the tall central portion of the existing Nunnykirk Hall. Dobson refaced this part and added lower wings to west and east which project forward and are linked by an Ionic colonnade. The western addition is terminated by a grand bow window while the east wing is carried back all along the east side of the house and forms the new entrance front. Here the details of the south colonnade reappear in the form of an Ionic screen and projecting *porte-cochère*. Indeed the horizontal line of the colonnades are carried all round the house and are one

28. Longhirst Hall, Northumberland, 1824—5. The hall

29. Longhirst Hall, Northumberland, 1824—5. Plasterwork in the drawing room

30. Nunnykirk Hall, Northumberland, 1825. The hall (by kind permission of Country Life)

31. Nunnykirk Hall, Northumberland, 1825

32. Meldon Park, Northumberland, 1832. Watercolour by Dobson and J.W. Carmichael (Laing Art Gallery, Newcastle upon Tyne)

30

31

32

of the elements which tie together the varied parts of the house. The other is the extensive use of banded rustication which covers the entrance front and the facades of the old house. This is a unique feature in Dobson's work and one that is more characteristic of his Durham friend and contemporary Ignatius Bonomi, whose Burn Hall of 1821-34 and Windlestone Hall of 1830-4 have banded rustication throughout. Bonomi's interest in French neo-classicism pervades his work and it must have been through Bonomi that this French characteristic made such a successful appearance in Dobson's work. A final touch of sophistication on the exterior is the unusual richness of the honeysuckle friezes which embellish the parapets.

Inside, the principal feature is a great hall reminiscent of that at Longhirst with a splendid ceiling of ornate coffered central dome and two segmental vaults. As we have come to expect, the quality of plasterwork is superb throughout.

The last classical house of importance in this period of Dobson's career is Meldon Park, begun in 1832 on a newly created estate purchased by Isaac Cookson III from the Greenwich Hospital Trust the same year[4]. Cookson was the third in a line of important Tyneside manufacturers and had taken charge of his father's glass interests to become one of the leading glass manufacturers in England and an important figure in Tyneside's chemical industry. Cookson had already employed Dobson in the late 1820s to lay out streets for development in Newcastle, and with the examples of Mitford, Longhirst and Nunnykirk all within 10 miles of his new estate, he would have needed no further evidence of Dobson's capabilities.

In plan, siting and design, Meldon is a typical Dobson classical house, though with no especially interesting features. The entrance front is a refined and elaborated version of Mitford. The portico is Ionic and deeper; the windows have moulded surrounds and the parapet is more delicate. The south front, with a splendid view across a terrace over the Wansbeck valley, has a canted bay in the centre. The east front is also a variation on that at Mitford; three closely spaced windows in the centre and a Wyatt window at either end. Dobson and Carmichael's watercolour illustrates how important Dobson felt the relationship between house and landscape to be. It shows the characteristic shrubbery protecting the entrance front and the dramatic placing of the south front, discreetly separated from the park by ha-ha and terrace, yet surrounded by woodland and pasture. The interiors, following the standard Dobson plan, are comparatively plain; the details less purely Greek and characterised by a restrained flamboyance more typical of the 1830s. The hall is very large with a grand staircase. Its comparative plainness was enriched between the wars with plasterwork and a new mahogany balustrade by Lutyens. The two drawing rooms lead into one another through double doors and into the library through a false bookcase.

Meldon has justifiably been described as the last flowering of the Georgian country house tradition. Like Dobson's earlier classical houses it combines neat but flexible planning with a deep appreciation of the relationship between the house and its setting, all contained within the discipline of the classical tradition.

If the 1830s saw a decline in commitment to the purity of the Greek Revival, it saw a burgeoning of interest in Gothic styles. This change was commented on at the beginning of this chapter and is readily evident in Dobson's own work. Indeed his first major Gothic house, Lilburn Tower in Northumberland can be considered a classical house in Gothic clothing, while he rapidly developed a mature if ultimately unimaginative Gothic style of his own in the years 1830-7.

Lilburn Tower is in all respects, except its architectural style, a perfect example of the Dobson country house of the 1820s[5]. Designed in 1828 for Henry Collingwood to replace an earlier house it is, as is to be expected, beautifully sited over the Lilburn burn, with the land dropping away sharply on two sides. The plan is once again the standard Dobson plan as seen at Longhirst and Meldon. The entrance front was, originally, perfectly symmetrical, as is the south, though the east front does not quite achieve symmetry. The service wing and conservatory are also placed in the 'appropriate' place.

In style Lilburn is a Tudor-Gothic amalgam typical of the period, but considerably more sophisticated than Dobson's Gothic efforts of only a few years earlier, for example, at West Jesmond House. The spikey angularity of those earlier designs has been replaced by a smoother compactness with a sophistication and accuracy of detail that is evidence not only of his increased knowledge of medieval prototypes, but also of the work of the two most fashionable proponents of Tudor-Gothic, William Wilkins and William Burn. Burn was two years younger than Dobson, but was by the 1820s already one of the most respected and successful country house architects in the country. Lilburn can be compared stylistically to a Burn house such as Ratho Park in Midlothian of 1824, though Burn's planning, for which he was so admired, has little in common with Dobson's at this stage.

33

33. Benwell Tower, Newcastle upon Tyne, 1830. An early proposal (R. N. McKellar and Partners)

34. Lilburn Tower, Northumberland, 1828. The dining room

34

It is a sad fact, in view of Dobson's self-proclaimed success in combating draughts in large houses, that he had to make major alterations to Lilburn Tower following its purchase by E. J. Collingwood of Chirton in 1843; the *porte-cochère* was moved to the left to enter the hall via a lobby and the great staircase was separated off from the hall. Inside there is an ensemble, unique in Dobson's work, of surviving fireplaces, fitted furniture, such as the library bookcases and the great oak dining room sideboard, and a largely unaltered decorative finish, especially the large areas of oak-grained plasterwork in the ceilings, of which that in the library is the most notable. The ceilings are heavily ribbed and encrusted with Gothic foliage, with Gothic versions of classical friezes around the cornice. Moreover there is a quantity of oak dining room, library and bedroom furniture original to the house and perhaps designed by Dobson himself. The generous staircase, which as at Longhirst was sited half way along the hall, is lit by an enormous mullioned and transomed window with excellent stained glass by William Wailes of Newcastle. The formality of the plan leads to few architectural surprises, but within a few years Dobson was to begin to exploit the picturesque possibilities of the Gothic style and in the next ten years made a series of designs in which he rapidly achieved a confident Gothic manner.

At Benwell Tower in 1830 he proposed substantial castellated Gothic additions to replace a decayed medieval house while retaining its substantial Georgian service wing. Early designs illustrate the incongruity of the juxtapostion, but also accentuate how Dobson has studiously avoided any symmetry in his own additions[6]. The composition is composed of several blocks carefully arranged to provide an irregular silhouette from every angle.

The Gothic style was particularly suited to the creation of picturesque compositions. Its admirers saw in the Tudor manor house, such as Compton Wynyates and Haddon Hall, an ideal of domestic architecture; picturesque, in that it 'looked good in a picture', also traditionally English and free from foreign influences, and capable of responding to the demands of efficient interior planning.

Dobson was well aware of these advantages:

'Whilst studying and sketching examples of Tudor architecture, I found that interior convenience was alone the object sought to be accomplished, and that much of the picturesque effect arose from chance. Much might be said of the advantages of Tudor architecture in the construction of buildings for domestic purposes, in producing varied and picturesque outlines, when the forms appear

35

36

to rise out of necessity; and I do not see that there can be any objection to adopting the decorated style of detail to a Tudor outline, provided it harmonises with the building. When this style is found to be too costly, then I have found what may be called the Manor House style, or irregular outline, a good substitute; and in some cases it will be found more in harmony with the component parts of the landscape.'7

37

35. Brinkburn Priory and Manor House, Northumberland, the latter 1831—7

36. Neasham Hall, Co. Durham, additions 1834—7

37. Beaufront Castle, Northumberland, 1837. The entrance front from an oil by J.W. Carmichael of 1843. (Laing Art Gallery, Newcastle upon Tyne)

The first master of picturesque architecture was John Nash whose best compositions arrange the main living rooms around a central hall, but projecting into the landscape to take advantage of views and create the necessary irregularity of skyline. This was Dobson's approach at Benwell Tower, though the service wing, incorporating the Georgian structure, makes no contribution to the picturesque effect. As built the house was a much simplified version of the first designs and consequently has a rather mean appearance, accentuated by the loss of its chimneys. However, considering the subsequent history of the house and its current use as a pub, the interiors are remarkably intact, with much dark stained oak panelling and heavily ribbed ceilings.

Contemporary with Benwell Tower, and rather more successful, are the additions Dobson made to Brinkburn Priory Manor House from 1831-7 for Major William Hodgson-Cadogan. The house, close to the roofless remains of Brinkburn Priory, had been built over part of the Monastic buildings and had been extended in 1810-11 by the Major's father in a plain Georgian 'Gothic' style. Dobson's work involved rebuilding the older part in his newly-mastered castellated Gothic manner. Despite the fact that no attempt was made to conform to the style of the church or the existing house, the additions are remarkably successful and contribute to the overall picturesqueness of the group, in their delightfully secluded setting on the River Coquet. The house contains the staircase from Anderson Place in Newcastle, installed by Dobson.

Further significant additions made by Dobson in the mid 1830s included a wing at Blenkinsopp Hall (1832-7 for Colonel Coulson), now demolished, and substantial remodelling of Neasham Hall in County Durham for Colonel James Cookson, a brother of Isaac Cookson of Meldon, made in 1834-7. Neasham appears to have been a late Georgian house of c.1800 to which Dobson made additions of the same scale as those at Nunnykirk; enclosing the house in Tudor wings with decorative gables,

38

38. Beaufront Castle, Northumberland, 1837. The garden front

39. Holme Eden, Cumbria. An early proposal for the south west front, c.1836 (RIBA)

40. Holme Eden, Cumbria, 1837. The entrance front

moving the entrance to the side and incorporating the plainer older portion by running an ornate parapet across the roof line. Neasham ended up as a very large house and was demolished in 1970.

Dobson's castellated Gothic designs climaxed in the late 1830s with the building of two large and impressive houses. Beaufront Castle[8], near Hexham in Northumberland, and Holme Eden, near Carlisle, were both begun in 1837 for families with successful manufacturing interests in the North of England.

William Cuthbert was a partner and major investor in the Cooksons' chemical and glass interests on Tyneside. In 1834 he began negotiating for part of the Beaufront estate, including the large late 17th and 18th century house, overlooking one of the most spectacular views in the Tyne Valley. The estate was finally purchased in 1836 and the new house begun in 1837. Dobson's house makes the most of the 'varied and picturesque outlines' produced by the Tudor Gothic style and from the east successfully evokes the low rambling composition of Haddon Hall. The house spreads out around a central tower and square stair turret placed over the main entrance. To its east a family wing was created in part of the remodelled old house; to the south the main block of the new house ironically reproduces the standard Dobson plan once again. However, it is so heavily disguised externally by a multitude of buttresses, oriels, bay windows and differing window and moulding details that it is only apparent internally. The only significant variation is the arrangement of entrance, hall and staircase. The hall is a Gothic extravagance and, although not a revival of the true medieval Great Hall as was being made by Pugin and Salvin elsewhere in the country at the same time, is an attempt to create 'instant history'. As Dobson and Carmichael's watercolour shows, by decorating it with hunting trophies, portraits of real or imaginary ancestors, suits of armour and displays of medieval arms, an impression of ancient lineage could be easily provided. However, the watercolour also illustrates the difficulty in finding a useful function for such a room. The early Victorians had more use for a billiard room than for displays of medieval pageantry. The staircase, too, is a fine vaulted space and the other reception rooms are well proportioned and lit with large windows. The ceilings are of conventional heavy ribs, that of the library superbly

39

40

grained to imitate oak. A rare surviving fireplace suggests they too were like those at Lilburn.

Holme Eden at Warwick Bridge, near Carlisle, is one of Dobson's least known large houses, but one of his most ambitious. In style it is almost identical to Beaufront, except for the use of the occasional gable and a heavier reliance on tall chimneys for vertical emphasis. It was built in a slightly simpler form than is shown in the drawings in the RIBA[9], and without the usually essential conservatory. The stone is the beautiful local red standstone.

The house was built for Peter Dixon of Peter Dixon and Sons, the largest cotton manufacturer in Carlisle with mills in Manchester, Carlisle and at Warwick Bridge itself. The firm had undergone great expansion in the 1820s and early 1830s and the Dixon family were near the height of their local influence. Peter was a Mayor of Carlisle in 1838-39, while his elder brother John was High Sheriff of Cumberland in 1838 and Mayor of Carlisle in 1840-41. The family were to provide Mayors throughout the 19th century.

41

The plan of Holme Eden is unique for Dobson at this time for being built around courtyards and for linking the various parts of the service accommodation with extensive corridors. The house thereby presents a compact whole in which house and service wing are not readily distinguishable externally. It is possible that the influence of William Burn is at work here; he too used courts and corridors to organise the complexity of the early Victorian country house. Like all Dobson's larger houses, Holme Eden is raised on a terrace, immediately above the river Eden and the surrounding woods and fields. The orientation is conventional: entrance to the west, main rooms along the south front and dining room to the east; service wing and stables around the courtyard to the north. What is unusual is the complete absence of a central hall. Instead there is a lobby leading indirectly to a long and wide corridor lit from the end and from a small court and leading through a door to a magnificent staircase, always a notable feature of these houses. Can this breaking up of the centralised 'Dobson' plan be an attempt to remove still more thoroughly the danger of draughts? If so, the result is aesthetically unsatisfactory; there is no sense of a natural centre or focus of the house, which is such an attractive feature of Dobson's other houses of this period.

However, Beaufront and Holme Eden, both remarkably unaltered, remain the best expressions of Dobson's brand of castellated Gothic domestic architecture. The days of the style were numbered by the criticisms of Pugin and Gilbert Scott, who ridiculed the fortified gatehouses and castellated parapets of houses which also boasted plate glass windows and large conservatories. In the following decades Dobson enters a period of bewildering variety in architectural style in which we seldom again find from him such commitment or quality.

41. Holme Eden, Cumbria, 1837. The staircase

Notes

1 For Mitford Hall see also *CL*, 17 February 1966.

2 *CL*, 17 February 1966.

3 *Ibid.*

4 *CL*, 24 February 1966.

5 *CL*, 8 November 1973.

6 Three elevations of "Design No 1" are with R.N. McKellar and Partners, Newcastle upon Tyne.

7 Wilkes, p.107.

8 *CL*, 29 January, 5 February 1976.

9 RIBA Drawings Collection G6/38 (1—3) previously called 'Benwell Tower'; here identified as being early designs for Holme Eden.

IV *The Spirit of Improvement: Public Architecture 1820-1840*

Town planning became an increasingly important part of an architect's work during the nineteeth century. In the previous century landowners in the most fashionable and prosperous cities, such as London, Bath and Edinburgh, had been developing land on the borders of the older parts of the cities to provide principally houses, but also shops, offices and public buildings. In many cases, they employed the best architects of their day, the brothers Adam were particular favourites, to design and carry out these speculative undertakings. Thus in Newcastle too, in the late 18th and early 19th centuries, population pressure on the crowded town encouraged many landowners to sell off fields as building plots. Westgate Hill and Hanover Square were created in this period, and Saville Row and Ridley Place extended the town eastwards. The degree to which these developments had architectural character depended on the landowner and on the Town Council, which required an Act of Parliament to create new streets and could specify the quality of the buildings to be erected. Small civic improvements had been made in the 18th century, the creation of Mosley Street and Dean Street in 1784 for example, but until the 1820s most new developments were privately financed and took place on the fringes of the town.

We have already noted Dobson's involvement in the selling of building land in Jesmond for Thomas Burdon in 1811 and 1814 — perhaps represented today by the part of Burdon Terrace to the east of Clayton Road. In the following years more sales of this kind were advertised through Dobson's office: in Chirton and North Shields (unsurprisingly), at Forth Banks, at Westgate and off the Shields turnpike at Wallsend, for example[1]. These were probably fairly modest unplanned developments; some may

42. The Fishmarket, Newcastle upon Tyne, 1823—6

43. Pandon Dene, Newcastle upon Tyne, 1821. From an engraving (Laing Art Gallery, Newcastle upon Tyne)

have come to nothing. Of more architectural interest were a proposal in 1817 for a crescent off Percy Street, not carried out, but perhaps reflected in the speculative 'projected street' on Oliver's 1830 map and the much later St. Thomas's Crescent development; the proposed formation in 1820 of a new road extending Jesmond Road in a straight line to the Great North Road, shortcutting the straggling Sandyford Lane and providing adjoining sites for villas; and the extensive new developments around Pandon Dene, across which John Stokoe's new bridge had been built in 1812.

Like the bridge over the Wear in Sunderland, the Pandon Dene Bridge opened up new land conveniently placed for the town centre and Dobson advertised the fact that building sites were available in this favourable location in 1813, 1815, 1823, 1824 and 1833. On the west side of the Dene, to be known as Picton Place, and on either side of New Bridge Street beyond the Dene were built villas, semi-detached and terraced houses of some architectural quality, some to designs by Dobson. He had, as we have already seen, built his own house in this newly fashionable street and similar neat Greek Revival villas overlooked the Dene in Picton Place, around the corner. Ridley Villas, on the north side of New Bridge Street east of the bridge, and the terrace opposite, are, with Dobson's house, the sole survivors of this rash of development. The semi-detached Ridley Villas, built on sites leased from Sir Matthew White Ridley, probably date from 1823 when Dobson was advertising sites for villas on the north side of New Bridge Street; they also may be to his design. By 1827 nine pairs had been built.

These building schemes around the bridge linked it to the newly extended Ellison Place, 'the genteelest and best built part of the town',[2] where Dobson was also active. Around 1825, he designed David Cram's large house at the end of the terrace, overlooking the Dene. This house merited a detailed description in Mackenzie's *History of Newcastle*[3]. He considered it 'noble and capacious' and 'the most chaste and elegant specimen of masonry exhibited in any private house in the town' and admired the quality of workmanship and the gardens, 'the whole ... designed by, and proceeding under the direction of, Mr. John Dobson, architect.' It must have been Dobson's most important town house and its loss has created an irreparable gap in our knowledge of his architecture. Rather later, around 1850, he closed the tree-lined street with Gresham Place, for the coal-owner James Morrison. All these activities resulted in what must have been, before the arrival of the Blyth and Tyne Railway in 1861-3, one of the most attractive residential parts of the town.

The same cannot be said of the new streets being laid out by Dobson at the opposite end of the town for Isaac Cookson Jnr[4]. Cookson was a leading Tyneside industrialist, being particularly involved in the glass industry. Dobson may have worked for the

44. Edward Street and Westgate Road, Newcastle upon Tyne, from 1827

Cooksons before, at their South Shields glassworks in 1817, but no solid evidence has come to light; more importantly, he was later to design one of his most important country houses, Meldon Park, for Isaac Cookson (see above p. 28).

At Westgate, on part of an estate he had acquired in the early 1820s, Cookson decided to sell off freehold building sites, in order, it has been suggested, to recoup his expenses in the contested Northumberland election of 1826. He employed Dobson to lay out the proposed streets and to design the elevations to which purchasers had to conform when building. From 1827 sites were sold at 19 guineas each, but were slow to sell. The terraces were named after Cookson's sons, John, Edward and William, and the whole 'village' named Arthur Hill. It is probable that some of the shorter streets above William Street, which included a pub The Cooksons' Arms, were also part of Cookson's estate. The terraces had some architectural character, being built with stone from Cookson's adjacent quarries, with projecting doorcases and an attempt at overall symmetry along the length of the terraces and in the ends of the terraces facing Westgate Hill. Unfortunately, we have little idea of what these terraces looked like in detail since they were cleared before the Second World War. Now only The Balmoral public house exists to remind us of the architectural pretentions of these early to mid 19th century streets.

Another nearby estate was to share the eventual sad fate of Arthur Hill. Thomas Anderson inherited on his uncle's death in 1831 not only the historic mansion of Anderson Place in the heart of Newcastle, but also other lands close to the town centre, in particular 30 acres of fields south of Westgate Hill, around what is now Blenheim Street. Anderson began to develop this land in 1834, the same year he sold Anderson Place to Richard Grainger (see below p.47), in the same manner as Cookson, that is by selling freehold plots to builders or other buyers, on a street plan laid out by Dobson. The houses were to be built to elevations supplied by Dobson and were to conform to a particular architectural standard. They had to be of brick with stone base, sills and window heads, stone cornice and stone doorcases. Despite the clearance of most of these houses during this century enough remain to give us an idea of their relatively humble yet classically derived facades.

The streets themselves were broad and the houses provided with gardens at the front and lanes at the back. The conditions of sale required that sewers were laid and that the back lanes were paved and provided with drains. However, in the great 1853 cholera epidemic the Westgate township was to have one of the worst death rates in Newcastle. One person in 57 died of cholera there; 30 in Blandford Street, 19 in Blenheim Street and 18 in George Street, streets which contributed most to the eventual toll of 291 deaths in the area. What had happened to these apparently elegant new streets in the suburbs of the town to have made them as desperately unhealthy as the ancient tenements on the Sandgate and the Quayside? Firstly, the builders had failed to carry out the Conditions of Sale; few drains and sewers were laid and little paving was carried out. Secondly, the Corporation had utterly failed to use the powers it had under the 1837 and 1846 Local Improvement Acts to force owners to bring their property up to the legal minimum standard. Thirdly, the houses themselves had rapidly become tenemented and overcrowded, because of a shortage of working-class and surplus of middle-class housing. The Report of the Cholera Inquiry Commissioners in 1854 did not hesitate to lay blame on the 'deliberate intentions' and 'criminal supidity' of the builders and on the gross inefficiency of the Council in making no attempt to improve matters, despite having full and specific powers to do so. Cookson's streets, for the same reasons, were also centres of the cholera outbreak.

Sadly, Dobson, when called as a witness to the Inquiry, was careful to distance himself from the problem, stating that 'small villas I have had very little to do with. It has generally been with buildings on a large scale', and, more evasively, when asked 'I think you said that you had not had much to do with building small houses here?', replied 'No'.

'Nor do you probably know much about them?'

'I do not at all'[5].

Yet in the 1820s, as we have seen, Dobson was deeply involved in the planning of just such developments at the west and east ends of the town. Dobson's apparent lack of familiarity with the requirements of a healthy water supply is evident also in his work on Gateshead's main sewer in 1849, built while a cholera epidemic raged in the town[6]. The sewer, however, was largely ineffective as it was of too wide a diameter to allow the water it carried to empty it thoroughly. Controversially, he considered it a great advantage to have the drainage of Newcastle and Gateshead directed straight into the Tyne.

Richard Grainger had been proud of the quality of water supply and sewerage in his

45

46

45. Newcastle General Cemetery, 1836. Chapels and north entrance

46. Eldon Square, Newcastle upon Tyne, 1825. From an etching after T.M. Richardson (Laing Art Gallery, Newcastle upon Tyne)

47. Whittle Dene Reservoir, Keeper's Cottage and Directors' Rooms, 1848

developments, and health and cleanliness became increasingly public concerns in the early 19th century. There had been public baths in Newcastle since at least 1781, but a subscription was opened in 1836 for shares in New Public Baths to designs by Dobson on the site of the present City Baths in Northumberland Road. However, part of them was shortly afterwards converted into an inn and they may not have been a great commerical success.

Cholera was also a factor in the decision to encourage the creation of new cemeteries in the 1820s and 1830s. Westgate Hill Cemetery had been opened in 1831 to designs by John and Benjamin Green while Dobson was probably responsible for laying out the new Gateshead Cemetery in 1834. But it was the Newcastle General Cemetery Company that employed Dobson in 1834-6 to create what is now recognised as one of his finest surviving works[7]. The Newcastle General Cemetery is triangular, bounded by a high stone wall. The south entrance is made through two massive gate piers of uncompromising severity. The north entrance is composed of two chapels, for Anglicans and Dissenters, which are Dobson's purest Greek Revival designs, of great originality and comparable with the work of the great German neoclassical architect, Schinkel. Here Dobson exploited the intrinsic character of Greek architecture, its noble monumentality and timelessness and employed to the best his own talents for scholarly detail, fine construction and, most importantly, superb architectural design. J.C. Loudon, who published several of Dobson's designs in his prolific architectural publications, and became an authority on cemetery design, particularly admired Dobson's entrance to the cemetery. Loudon would have approved too of the layout and planting within it, though not, as James Stevens Curl has remarked, of the weeping willows. However it is, with its numerous excellent classical funerary monuments and mature trees, the North East's finest Victorian cemetery. It is an architectural memorial in more ways than one for it contains the graves not only of John Dobson himself but of his architectural contemporaries William Stokoe, Thomas Oliver and John Green.

The Whittle Dene Water Company of which Richard Grainger was a director, provided Newcastle's first clean water supply from reservoirs near Welton in Northumberland. Dobson designed the pretty little 'keeper's cottage and Directors' Rooms' overlooking the reservoirs in 1848 and may have had some involvement in the engineering of a later small reservoir[8].

In contrast to his denial of association with the building of small houses, Dobson, in his evidence to the Cholera Inquiry Commissioners, was happy to claim responsibility for Eldon Square, the sort of urban architecture he was prouder to have been

47

associated with. Eldon Square was indeed remarkable, the first formal town planning scheme in Newcastle and the first in the Corporation's 19th century ventures into large-scale town improvement. The scheme originated with the creation of Blackett Street in 1824, just beyond and parallel to the town wall. Previously the street had consisted of 'a few straggling houses and workshops... the street, being unpaved, was dirty and almost impassable... a useless waste, where manure was deposited'[9]. Dobson had surveyed and valued the old street for the Blacketts, on whose land it lay, as early as 1815[10], and Mackenzie, who was writing at the time of building and with information supplied by Dobson, attributes the design of the houses in Blackett Street to Dobson. Thomas Oliver, however, claimed[11] that the Council had originally commissioned plans for Blackett Street and Eldon Square from him and drawings and a model had been submitted. Dobson had been asked for his opinion and on receiving his proposed alterations the Council decided to build Eldon Square to Dobson's elevations. Oliver states that Blackett Street was built to his own designs and plans. It is at any rate clear that Dobson was responsible for the facades of Eldon Square, facades which contributed greatly to the Square's distinction not just in Newcastle, but nationally. Unlike most large urban developments of the Regency period, such as John Nash's contemporary Regent's Park terraces, Eldon Square was characterised by high quality ashlar masonry rather than stucco, one of the earliest use of stone for domestic architecture in Newcastle. In addition, Eldon Square was comparatively plain and undecorated, with the notable exception of the Greek honeysuckle motifs in the cast iron balconies. In the true neoclassical maner, the angles of the three terraces that composed the Square were accented with shallow Doric pilasters, and the centre of the north side was stressed with a higher roofline and, in the original design, though unbuilt, an Ionic portico. The design seems an unconscious echo of David Stephenson's North Shields Market Place, but dressed in the severer clothes of the Greek Revival. The centre of the Square was filled with an ornamental garden for the use of residents.

The builder of Eldon Square and Blackett Street, and the man on whom the commercial risk of the venture rested, was Richard Grainger. For the next fifteen years it was to be impossible to separate the architectural developments of Newcastle from the ambitions, financial skills and enthusiasms of this man[12]. Unlike Dobson, ten years his senior, Grainger was of the most humble origins, having been the son of a Quayside porter who died when his son was thirteen, and of an 'industrious, clever and neat handed' mother, who supported her family by washing, starching and glove making. Grainger had a respectable schooling and an apprenticeship with a builder and house-carpenter. Success as a builder on his own account and a profitable marriage gave him the resources to undertake the Eldon Square project with confidence. What cannot be doubted was his desire to see the town benefit commercially, culturally and architecturally from his speculations. In 1827 he made available a site in Blackett Street for T.M. Richardson and H.P. Parker's Northern Academy of Arts, built to Dobson's designs for £2,000. About the same time he leased 'on liberal and favourable terms' a further site for the Library of the Literary, Scientific and Mechanical Institution, opened in 1828. The Northern Academy of Arts had a first floor portico *in antis*, i.e. recessed flush with the facade, in a style echoing that of John Shaw's Cresswell Hall of 1820-4 (see above p.24). The Literary, Scientific and Mechanical Institution, a less familiar building, had a rather more elegant facade, though it was of stucco rather than stone. There is no direct evidence that Dobson was the architect, but he was a full member of the Institute's Governing Committee and lectured to its members.

In the same period Dobson was also engaged in some other public buildings. For Newcastle's Common Council he made a semicircular addition to the east end of the Guildhall to replace the ancient decayed Maison de Dieu, originally a charity almshouse, but by then used as a Quayside warehouse. Dobson's addition consisted of a new covered fishmarket, a new Merchants' Court and offices for the town clerk, his deputy and the prothonotary and a fire-proof room for the Corporation records. It was built from 1823-6 and comprised a bold semicircular colonnade, with two stories of offices above, joined to the late 18th century neoclassicism of William Newton and David Stephenson's Guildhall of 1796. Despite the fishwives' initial lack of enthusiasm for their new market, the building was considered 'one of the handsomest architectural ornaments of the town which has cleared the Sandhill of the number of fishstalls and widened the entrance to the Quay'[13]. Inside the Merchant Adventurers' Court Dobson refitted their 17th century carved oak panelling and elaborate fireplace and concocted a new cornice and ceiling in early 17th century style, with a fictitious date of 1620. His double-glazed windows were considered an innovation.

While the Fishmarket was building, Dobson added to Newton's Newcastle Lunatic Asylum in 1824 and the next year designed his first important public building in the Gothic style, the Lying-in Hospital in New Bridge Street. Dobson gave his plans for this charitable 'asylum for poor married pregnant women' free and they do not speak of great confidence in the Gothic style. The building is a rectangular block with hipped roof, the facade of ashlar with windows and niches in an unhappy mixture of Decorated and Perpendicular styles and weakly arranged. The side elevations of the

Northern Academy of Arts

NEWCASTLE UPON TYNE.

48

building are of coursed rubble with plain rectangular windows with Tudor drip mouldings. The individual elements are well detailed and based on observation of medieval originals, but the whole is unconvincingly composed.

By far the most important civic enterprise with which Dobson was concerned at this time was the new Gaol and House of Correction at Carliol Square, Newcastle, built between 1823 and 1828 at the cost of a little over £35,000[14]. His plans were selected from a number of competing designs by the Gaol Committee of the Common Council in October 1822, but the choice must have been a foregone conclusion since Dobson had accompanied the prime mover of the scheme, the municipal reformer and Mayor of Newcastle Archibald Reed, on a fact finding visit to London in December 1818, and in July 1820 attended a meeting of the Gaol Committee to advise its members on possible designs. The decision to build a new prison had been formally taken earlier that year after the old gaol in the New Gate (demolished 1823) had been criticised at the Spring Assizes as 'insufficient, insecure, inconvenient, too small and out of repair'. At first the Castle Garth was favoured as a site for the new complex, and Dobson seized on the opportunity to propose a substantial scheme of improvement which would have cleared surrounding property and converted the old castle into a debtors' prison, with a new gateway to the south east, linking to a governor's house, magistrates' hall, gaol and house of correction, all in a castellated style and enclosed by corner towers and an encircling wall. A new street was to have connected with St. Nicholas's Church, and as Mackenzie observed, 'the county courts, the old Castle, the new prisons, and St. Nicholas' steeple, would have presented an incomparably grand and imposing group'[15]. The Council were too timid to accept this plan, probably on grounds of expense, though for a time were even prepared to consider the dubious idea of having the house of correction within the Castle Garth and the gaol elsewhere. Ultimately they decided on an entirely new but controversial site at the south end of Carliol Croft, now Carliol Square.

During the late 18th and early 19th centuries many prisons were being built as a result of the general impetus towards public improvement, specifically influenced by philanthopists such as John Howard who had thoroughly investigated gaols in Britain and Europe and argued ceaselessly for more humane conditions capable of improving rather than degrading a criminal's moral worth. Most new designs represented a major advance on the old system of manacled prisoners huddled together in a single space or confined indiscriminately in insanitary cells. They embodied more modern and sophisticated notions of correction and reform reflecting the rationalist virtues of the Enlightenment, and in particular the idea of classification, whereby different classes of prisoner were separated according to sex, age and the nature of the crime. As a result such plans tended to be especially typical of public architecture during the neoclassical age, being extremely ordered, and geometrically arranged; some were variations of the Greek cross system favoured by Howard himself, others were radiating or concentric designs influenced by the 'Panopticon', an all purpose if ultimately impractical proposal formulated by the philosopher Jeremy Bentham in 1791. This extended the idea of surveillance to an extreme degree, consisting of a masonry cylinder with cells arranged around the outside walls and partitions radiating from a central inspection tower[16].

Dobson addressed the problem with characteristic thoroughness, studying other examples of prison design such as Liverpool, which he admired, and Edinburgh, where the circular arrangement of cells gave too much opportunity for the inmates to converse. He also canvassed the opinions of prison governors and other experts on his plan, and would certainly have been aware of the 'Panopticon' idea. Another influence might have been the Millbank Penitentiary, then under construction on concentric lines, which he must surely have seen during his London visit with Archibald Reed to examine the famous Newgate Gaol, built by George Dance between 1769 and 1778.

The most up to date concepts of punishment, security and reform were reflected in Dobson's Newcastle Gaol design. It consisted of a horseshoe shaped central block containing offices and supervisors' rooms, linked to a gatehouse and overlooking six radiating wings (of which only five were initially built) forming a semi-circular complex closed off by a double wall, which created a garden, exercise courts, and yards. There are minor discrepancies between the plan published by Mackenzie illustrated here and Dobson's original design[17], but it is clear that the central block was flanked by two slightly larger wings (all had a length, 66 feet, equivalent to the width of the central block) one for debtors and one for the most hardened criminals. The remaining four radiating wings as proposed were identical cell blocks giving separate accommodation for males and females, and with cells arranged on one side only (alternating floor by floor) thus preventing communication or view between the

48. The Northern Academy of Art, Newcastle upon Tyne, 1827. From an engraving (Newcastle Central Library)

49. The Lying-in Hospital, Newcastle upon Tyne, 1825

blocks; these were further separated by dividing walls. Construction was of stone with intermediate floors supported by iron columns, as advocated for the 'Panopticon', to reduce the risk of fire. The result was an outstandingly original design, combining the merits of a radiating scheme with the main features of London's Newgate Gaol, a central block with flanking wings. The overwhelming visual severity of the Carliol Square Prison, though more like a feudal fortress than Dance's awe-inspiring classical design, also continued the current tradition of symbolic or associational expression in architecture, through the choice of 'appropriate' styles and forms.

Dobson's other major prison schemes were also produced at about this time. In 1821 he won a competition for the design of the Northumberland gaol, house of correction and sessions house at Morpeth. Built (1822-28) like its Newcastle counterpart of local stone and equivalent in scale, size and cost, it was more authentically castellated in style — the architect himself stated that Conway, Beaumaris and Caernarvon Castles had inspired the design[18] — with a plan largely based upon the concept of the medieval castle keep and curtain wall. Thus the horseshoe shaped structure, developed into the central feature of the Newcastle design, which had not needed to incorporate a court house, is here combined into a gigantic gatehouse 72 feet high containing a porter's lodge with a monumental staircase leading to a sessions house above. Although now converted to a different use this survives largely intact as a splendid semicircular space with gallery and rib vaulted ceiling. The rather simplified quasi-medieval detailing of this and other surviving rooms resembles that of Dobson's contemporary Gothic country houses. Under the sessions house an arched entrance led via a court to a central building, part of which survives, containing offices and the governor's house, and overlooking a nine sided polygonal court with vaulted cells facing inwards around most of the perimeter to the left and right. Again the complex was surrounded by a double range of walls.

A comparison of Morpeth and Newcastle gaols, two of the most important designs of Dobson's whole career, suggests that he was influenced also by that most famous of European prisons, the 'Maison de Force' at Ghent. Begun in 1773 it incorporated eight trapezium shaped courts joined to each side of a central octagon, with cells (arranged in this case back to back) placed around the circumference and along the divisions between the courts; it was described by Howard in several of his works. The Morpeth and Newcastle designs, minus the gatehouse element, would if combined closely resemble the plan of the 'Maison de Force'.

At this time Dobson was also commissioned to make additions to the Hexham House of Correction (1822) which he executed in the severest block-like style, and the following year designed small prisons at Belford and Wooler, Northumberland. The Belford example survives and is an informal neo-Tudor building, unexpectedly domestic in type. More importantly, Dobson had won a competition in March 1822 for the design of the Carlisle County Gaol. Soon afterwards, however, his plans were rejected on the advice of John Orridge, the Governor (and designer) of Bury St. Edmunds Gaol, which was a fully developed radial type. A completely new design formulated by William Nixon in consultation with Orridge, an internationally respected expert, was substituted; this was further modified after Nixon's death by Christopher Hodgson and the building completed in Gothic style in 1827[19]. No trace can be found of Dobson's design, but it was almost certainly castellated and probably resembled his Morpeth plan. Its rejection may well have been a further reason for Dobson to adopt the radiating principle, at least in part, in his Newcastle scheme.

By the mid 1820s, the spirit of improvement was flourishing as never before. Eneas Mackenzie, who clearly had Dobson's advice on all aspects of architectural activity, devoted a whole chapter of his *History of Newcastle* to 'Improvements Effected and Projected' and described in detail several extravagant proposals[20]. One, 'according to the plans... by Mr. Dobson', was to continue Blackett Street in a straight line across Gallowgate, eventually joining the Carlisle turnpike; another, soon abandoned, was to continue the line of villas at Picton Place in a bold sweep to Vine Lane along the banks of Pandon Dene; a third was to continue Trafalgar Street down to the Pandon Burn and thence to the Quayside, thus providing a further and gentler means of ascent from the river to the higher parts of the town. It is interesting that the first and third of these schemes appear as proposals on Thomas Oliver's 1830 map. In the same map Oliver also partially adopted Dobson's plans, described in detail by Mackenzie, to exploit the open spaces of Anderson Place and The Nuns.

The thirteen acres of ground attached to the Elizabethan mansion of Anderson Place had once been the seat of the Blacketts and was a unique feature to find within the walls of a town. In 1783 the Blacketts had offered the house to the Corporation, who felt unable to purchase it perhaps because of their simultaneous involvement in

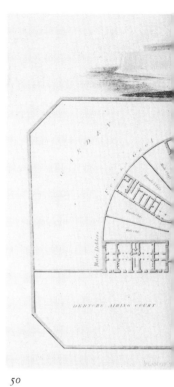

50

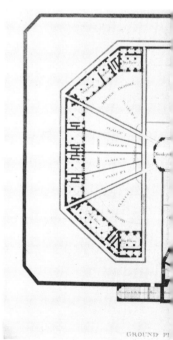

51

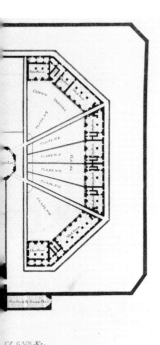

one of their rare 18th century enterprises, the creation of Mosley and Dean Streets. The rejection was lamented by Mackenzie who no doubt hoped, with Dobson, that the detailed publication of the latter's grand and ambitious scheme would help to bring about its fulfilment.

Dobson proposed that on the site of Anderson Place itself should be built a mansion house with 'four handsome stone fronts, the north, south and west sides to rise from a bold terrace; and the latter to be ornamented with eight beautiful pillars. The east front to face Pilgrim Street, and to have a lofty grand portico, capable of admitting carriages.'[21] With the sensitive eye of the landscape gardener, he proposed retaining the avenue of trees leading from Pilgrim Street to Anderson Place as part of the ceremonial approach to this new 'civic palace'.

To the west of the Mansion House was to be a large open market place bounded by four wide new streets lined with new buildings. These streets were carefully planned to make the most of existing features in the town: the west street was to run from Blackett Street, opposite and perpendicular to the centre of Eldon Square, to the junction of Newgate and the Bigg Market, then a severe bottleneck; the east street began at the junction of Blackett Street and High Friar Street, ran in front of the Mansion House and into High Bridge opposite the then New Butcher Market, which was to be given a more imposing entrance. The north and south bounds of the new square ran off Pilgrim Street on either side of the Mansion House, towards Newgate Street. However, these proposed streets had no impact on the town beyond the area bounded by Blackett Street, Pilgrim Street, High Bridge Street and Newgate Street.

Dobson's plan for the exploitation of Anderson Place and its grounds would undoubtedly have resulted in a most splendid centrepiece for the town, even if limited in its scope. That it was not built and was eventually superseded by Grainger's successful and substantially different proposal reflects Dobson's lack of financial and Council backing and probably the scheme's lack of commercial viability. Compared to Grainger's, it seems to have lacked sufficient street frontage and building area. Moreover, Grainger included several additional public buildings in his plan and, although it echoes some of Dobson's ideas, it takes into account to a greater extent the geography of the town. A more detailed discussion of Grainger's scheme and of Dobson's involvement in it must wait until later. In the meantime, three of Dobson's proposed new streets appeared in John Wood's 1827 map and one, that leading off Eldon Square, is shown as a 'Projected Street' on Oliver's 1830 map, thus keeping at least part of the scheme alive[22].

In 1829 Oliver achieved his first major architectural success by designing Leazes Terrace for Grainger. Leazes Terrace is over twice the length of any of the Eldon Square ranges and is more heavily decorated, with fluted Corinthian pilasters at the corners and a richly decorated frieze. It was built on Grainger's own land and was a

50. Gaol and House of Correction, Newcastle upon Tyne, 1822—8. From a plan published in Mackenzie, 1827

51. Northumberland Gaol, House of Correction and Sessions House, Morpeth, 1821—8. Plan as published in Mackenzie, 1827

52. Northumberland Gaol, House of Correction and Sessions House, Morpeth, 1821—8. Gatehouse as surviving

53

building speculation of magnificent proportions, the most splendid 19th century terraced development outside John Nash's contemporary Metropolitan Improvements in London.

While Leazes Terrace and indeed Eldon Square were still under construction, Grainger was undertaking yet another major speculation. In 1830 he sent to Newcastle's Common Council plans and a model of a proposed Corn Exchange to be built on land he had acquired in Pilgrim Street opposite the end of Mosley Street. The building, designed by Dobson, was to cost just over £5,000 excluding an ornamental stone front. However, we know that Dobson had previously, around 1825, made plans for a Corn Exchange on a site occupied by the 'ancient and crazy dwellings' of Middle Street, between the Groat Market and the Cloth Market[23]. The designs were probably made for a private consortium which had been negotiating with the Council for approval to build such a new Corn Market. A covered Corn Market was evidently a very much needed public improvement, but there were to be years of argument between the various interested parties within and outside the Council before one was eventually built in 1838 on the Middle Street site, to John and Benjamin Green's designs, though left uncompleted. What Dobson's earlier design looked like we do not know, except that, in Mackenzie's ambiguous words, its entrance was to consist of 'a noble colonnade, executed in a simple and grand style, to harmonise with the architecture of the adjoining Christian temple,' i.e. St. Nicholas's Church. Grainger was set against the Middle Street site; as late as 1838 he was offering the Central Exchange site free to the Council, for use as a Corn Exchange, despite a committee of the Council having in February 1831 decided on the Middle Street location in preference to Grainger's earlier Pilgrim Street offer.

Grainger was committed to erecting a major public building on the rejected site. In June 1831 work began on the Royal Arcade and finished, almost miraculously, in May 1832. As a Corn Exchange the site would seem to have had distinct advantages, being near to the quayside, but also close to the other principal markets, the New Butcher Market to the north of Mosley Street, and the older markets opposite St. Nicholas's. Instead, Grainger decided to create a shopping arcade, a fashionable building type not yet seen in Newcastle, but common in London and Paris[24]. Architecturally the Royal Arcade was a major contribution to Newcastle's public architecture and one that well deserved the presentation to Grainger of a silver tureen and salver at a public dinner held in his honour in July 1833. The arcade itself was based closely on the highly successful Lowther Arcade in London by Witherden Young of 1830 which itself was held to surpass the famous Burlington Arcade. In its turn, Newcastle's Royal Arcade was considered to be superior, particularly in its lighting, to the Lowther Arcade, and

54

53. Northumberland Gaol, House of Correction and Sessions House, Morpeth, 1821—8. Interior of Sessions House

54. Royal Arcade, Newcastle upon Tyne, 1831—2. The interior from an engraving. (Laing Art Gallery, Newcastle upon Tyne)

thus to be the finest in the country. It was 250 feet long and 20 feet wide, floored with chequered stone and black marble and containing 16 shops. Lighting was by eight conical skylights set in domes.

The Royal Arcade was the first to be built as part of a self-contained commercial development. The Arcade was a single vast building containing in addition to the shopping arcade, banks, auction rooms, professional offices, Government offices and a Post Office and a steam and vapour bath. The front to Pilgrim Street dominated the eighteenth century houses of the street rising to a height of 75 feet with giant Corinthian columns above a severe Doric ground floor. A heavily ornamented cornice, a balustraded attic storey and a coat of arms by Dunbar lay above. A similar block at the far end of the Arcade at a lower level faced Manor Chare.

The Arcade did, however, have commercial problems. Shops were still unlet in 1841 when Collard and Ross[25] recognised that the exit to Manor Chare discouraged the use of the Arcade as a thoroughfare, a desirable attribute; the most successful arcades were U-shaped, or led from one fashionable shopping street to another. The Post Office moved out in the 1860s and demolition was first proposed in the 1880s, when Manor Chare was described as 'an unsavoury neighbourhood'. It was eventually lost in the early 1960s, blackened and derelict. The Fine Art Commission's recommendation that the facade be rebuilt close to its original site was not carried out. The Arcade's commercial failure must lie at Grainger's feet; architecturally it amounted to one of Dobson's most dignified compositions, showing his mastery of bold large scale forms, not perhaps to be surpassed until his early designs for Newcastle's Central Station fifteen years later.

The climax of Dobson's association with Richard Grainger was the work he did for Grainger's major redevelopment in the centre of Newcastle, centred on the Anderson Place site. Grainger presented his plan, notably different from Dobson's earlier scheme of c.1825, to the Common Council in May 1834 while in negotiation with Thomas Anderson over the purchase of Anderson Place. The plan was soon published, was briefly controversial on account of its effect on property prices in the lower part of the town, but was by mid July 1834 overwhelmingly approved by popular acclaim and by the Common Council itself. Essential to the latter's approval was the support and advice Grainger had from the solicitor, John Clayton, Newcastle's Town Clerk since 1822. The story of Grainger's great enterprise which resulted in 'the best designed city in England' has been well told elsewhere, particularly by Wilkes and Dodds[26]. It is clear that Grainger had architects working in his office full time who probably laid out the streets and designed most of them. John Walker and George Wardle seem to have been most active in this respect (when setting up on their own account in 1841, they said they had worked for Grainger since 1834). John and Benjamin Green were architects of the new Theatre Royal and for the rest of the block between Market Street and Shakespeare Street. Dobson's designs seem to have been confined to the new Markets[27], perhaps including their street elevations, and the east side of Grey Street between Shakespeare Street and Mosley Street[28]. There is no evidence of Thomas Oliver's involvement; the rest of the street elevations must have been the responsibility of Wardle and Walker.

For the most part the streets are plain and untheatrical, certainly when compared with John Nash's contemporary Metropolitan Improvements, and have the advantage over them in being solidly built in finely carved stone rather than cheaper painted stucco. The excellence of the design is in the careful way each range is composed with balancing central and terminal emphases. The highlights are the Theatre Royal and the Central Exchange triangle with its three domed corners.

Dobson's portion of Grey Street is notably distinct in design from the typical Wardle and Walker pattern. In some respects Dobson's is heavier and coarser, but it is also more varied, more three dimensional; less elegant perhaps, but more characterful.

Grey Street was not completed until 1837 and its termination, the Grey Monument, for which Dobson had unsuccessfully submitted a design, was erected in 1838; the Markets, however, were the first part of the scheme to be finished, having been opened on 24th October 1835, within one year of the contract being signed. The building cost the Corporation £36,290, less the £15,000 which Grainger had paid for the Corporation's old Flesh Market, south of High Bridge. Dobson's enormous covered market, the largest in the country, was divided into two parts, an open-plan Vegetable Market, 318 feet by 57 feet, with a complex roof structure designed originally without the cast iron pillars inserted apparently at the request of the Corporation's architects, and a Butcher Market housed in a network of avenues and arcades with classical detailing. The whole was contained within four streets of shops and houses 'surpassing anything in street architecture hitherto witnessed in this neighbourhood'[29], a foretaste of the quality of Grainger's street architecture elsewhere.

The 1820s and '30s saw other streets being laid out and built up in Newcastle and beyond. Neville Street was planned by Dobson in 1828, to link the commercial centre of the town to the rapidly developing west end, and opened in 1835; St. Mary's Place, designed by Dobson as his only non-classical street to complement his church of St. Thomas's opposite, was being built from 1829.

Stately terraces along the Great North Road of the 1830s and 1840s, Jesmond Terrace, St. Mary's Terrace (the only one remaining), St. Thomas's Place and Jesmond High Terrace can be attributed to Dobson, as can Carlton Terrace on the north side of Jesmond Road, itself first proposed by Dobson in 1820, but probably not laid out until the 1830s. Carlton Terrace dates from c.1840 and is a late example of a terraced residential development treated as an architectural whole with a projecting and slightly raised centre and wings. Shallow Doric pilasters, and paired brackets are the only remaining classical details, but the composition is in a tradition that originated over 100 years earlier in John Wood's Queen Square at Bath of 1729. At North Shields Dobson had surveyed land between Tynemouth and the present Linskill Terrace for William Linskill as early as 1816 for proposed housing development[30]. This having been achieved in the following decades, in 1860 Dobson designed crescents in the same area, east of Washington Terrace, for the same family[31]. Overlooking the sea at Tynemouth, Percy Gardens was laid out in 1839 close to his Crown Hotel and public baths; Dobson was probably also responsible for the group of streets around Prior's Terrace, close to his later Collingwood Monument. Tynemouth was entering a period of rapid growth encouraged by the creation of the railway link from Newcastle.

At Monkwearmouth in the 1830s, the Wear Bridge was still encouraging growth north of the river where Sir Hedworth Williamson was developing his land. Dobson laid out Bonner's Field in 1835, a new street linking the bridge to Sir Hedworth's North Quay, built a small dock office at his North Dock in about 1837 and later laid out several residential streets north of Dame Dorothy Street for the same patron. At nearby Roker, where industry gave way to recreation, Dobson designed another group of hotel, terrace and baths for the Abbs family. Shares in the Monkwearmouth Bath Company were obtainable through Dobson's office.

Dobson's other important County Durham patron was Lord Londonderry who, with Lord Lambton, was one of the richest landowners in the county. Their wealth originated with coal and between them the two families owned over half the coal shipped from Sunderland around 1820. Lord Londonderry was determined to save the harbour dues at Sunderland by building his own harbour on land he had just acquired at Seaham. To complement this he invited John Dobson to design a new town[32]. Initial

55. St. Thomas's Place and Jesmond High Terrace, Newcastle upon Tyne, 1830s

consultations took place in 1823 but by the time the foundation stones of the harbour and town were laid in November 1828 Dobson's proposals had already been largely abandoned. Londonderry was determined not to invest money in the town when it was more urgently needed for the harbour. So Dobson's design, delicately Italianate, with the railway running down to the harbour beneath the colliery offices, and flanked by an hotel, shopping area, and two large stone built crescents, with workers' houses behind, was not carried out. The street plan was revised and leaseholds were sold haphazardly with little enforcement of architectural standards. Londonderry's resources were being spent on the harbour, which cost over £118,000, and on the massive rebuilding of Wynyard Park.

Notes

1 Numerous newspaper references collected in A.G. Chamberlain, *North East Architects and the Building Trade to 1865: References in local newspapers*, 1986 (typescript deposited in Newcastle Central Library) have been invaluable in identifying Dobson's lesser activities, many examples of which follow.

2 Mackenzie, 1827, I, p.190.

3 *Ibid.*

4 W.R. Foster, *Some notes on house building in Newcastle upon Tyne, 1820—1860*, 1981 (typescript deposited in Newcastle Central Library), provided several details for the following account.

5 *Report of the Cholera Inquiry Commissioners*, 1854, p.311.

6 F.W. Rogers, 'Gateshead and the Public Health Act of 1848', *AA*, 4, XLIX, pp.153ff.

7 *CL*, 2 July 1981, pp.68—9.

8 R.W. Rennison, *Water to Tyneside*, 1979, p.57.

9 Mackenzie, 1827, p.188.

10 NCRO (ZBL 62/4).

11 Oliver, p.97.

12 For a detailed account of Grainger's activities see Wilkes and Dodds.

13 Mackenzie, 1827, p.217.

14 See the Minutes of the Gaol Committee, TWA (279/1).

15 Mackenzie, 1827, p.203.

16 For a discussion of late eighteenth and early nineteenth century prisons, see T. Markus, "Pattern of the Law", *The Architectural Review*, vol. 116, no. 694, October 1954.

17 The drawings are in TWA (279/1).

18 Wilkes, p.107.

19 Reported in the *Carlisle Patriot*, 3 March and 17 August, 1822.

20 Mackenzie, 1827, pp.197ff.

21 Mackenzie, 1827, pp.200—201.

22 Curiously, Dobson announced in the *Newcastle Courant* on 7 January 1826 that 'Major Anderson has been induced to divide the said field [Nun's Field] into sites for let'. But no development seems to have followed.

23 Mackenzie, 1827, pp.199—200.

24 Margaret Mackeith, *The History and Conservation of Shopping Arcades*, 1986, pp104-5.

25 Collard and Ross, pp.63—64.

26 Wilkes and Dodds, pp.56—102.

27 Perspectives in the Laing Art Gallery, Newcastle upon Tyne.

28 Perspective in the Laing Art Gallery, Newcastle upon Tyne, and elevations and plans in the Getty Museum, California.

29 *NJ*, 31 October, 1835.

30 NCRO (ZMD 68/7).

31 NCRO (ZMD 68/5).

32 Mackenzie and Ross, 1834, II, p.374, and Seaham Community Association, *History of Seaham*, 1985, p.81. Drawings in DCRO (D/Lo/E 596 (386)).

V Chapels and Churches 1820-1862

At the present time Dobson is justly celebrated as a classicist and particularly for his country house designs; his ecclesiastical architecture is less wholeheartedly admired. Yet in his own day the situation was almost the reverse. He was regarded as a pioneer of Gothic (the principal church style of the 19th century) who had made a substantial study of English medieval forms, and as an ecclesiastical architect 'par excellence'[1].

Our reservations stem from the fact that his work in this field mirrors the aesthetic uncertainties of the period in which he lived; Dobson can be categorised neither as a thoroughly Georgian architect nor as a proper representative of the High Victorian age. Also, he worked at a time of population growth when, in addition to thousands of new churches being built, innumerable older ones were altered or 'improved', a practice in which Dobson was very much involved; in this his work is seen to reflect an approach which began to be discredited even in his own lifetime and which would be totally unacceptable today. However, from the very start ecclesiastical architecture became a consistently important theme in Dobson's long career, representing numerically more than a quarter of his work.

His early classical phase reached a climax in 1825-26 with the neo-Greek rectangularity of St. James's Presbyterian Chapel, Blackett Street, Newcastle. Here Dobson adapted Christian worship to the temple form, but the interior was arranged more like a small theatre with seating placed in a semicircle and a gallery above. After this, his essays in classicism for church design were extremely rare. His unbuilt proposal for a new chapel at Elswick (1838-40) would have been, however, an interesting synthesis of Greek and Roman forms, while his Presbyterian Church, North Shields (1856-57) is an excellent example of his later Italianate mode.

During the 1820s the Victorian Gothic Revival was yet to come, but medieval building was being studied more and more. It was no longer seen as a decorative novelty but as something worthy of the same archaeological attention that Greek

56. Archibald Reed Monument, Newcastle General Cemetery, 1843

57. Design for a proposed chapel at Elswick, 1838—40. From a drawing by Dobson (Newcastle University Library)

architecture had already received. Thus, among the richly illustrated folios published as source material for architects and connoisseurs alike were John Carter's *Ancient Architecture of England* (1807), John Britton's *The Architectural Antiquities of Great Britain* (1804-14), and the latter's fourteen volume *Cathedral Antiquities of Great Britain* (1814-35). Even more authoritative was Augustus Charles Pugin's *Specimens of Gothic Architecture* (1821-23). Meanwhile, in the more popular journals like *The Gentleman's Magazine* articles had begun to appear calling for the more accurate and sensitive restoration of medieval work and it was with the same purpose that the architect Thomas Rickman published *An Attempt to Discriminate the Styles of English Architecture* in 1817. Like Dobson and many other architects of the time, Rickman seems to have had equal liking for both Greek and Gothic styles, but wished to facilitate modern Gothic church design. He divided English medieval architecture into four main phases — 'Norman', 'Early English', 'Decorated', and 'Perpendicular' — thus providing a vocabulary of identification still in use today.

From an early age Dobson seems to have developed a similar antiquarian approach; as a youth he made measured drawings of the tower of St. Nicholas's Church, Newcastle, and of mouldings and tracery at Tynemouth Priory. Drawings he made of the Old Keep, Newcastle, were to prove useful many years later for restoration work. As a young architect, if hardly the originator of the Gothic Revival as some have claimed, he developed this more than ordinary interest in medieval architecture by travelling in England, Wales and France, sketching assiduously, and continued over the years to make studies of this kind. He built up a collection of architectural fragments from buildings demolished or restored, including an original pinnacle from the tower of St. Nicholas's Church which he replaced in 1827, and two stone piers from the Hospital of St. Mary the Virgin, Newcastle (demolished 1844)[2]. Dobson joined the Society of Antiquaries of Newcastle upon Tyne as early as 1815, and by the 1820s is to be found giving public lectures on the history of architecture to other local groups. He is known to have possessed at least one treatise on Greek art and design[3], and it seems highly likely that he was familiar with the kind of scholarly publication of medieval architecture mentioned above. Certainly opportunities to work in the Gothic style soon came his way.

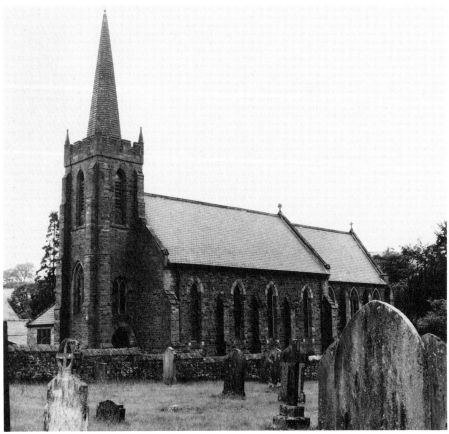

In 1818 he restored the medieval church of St. John Lee, near Hexham, and a year earlier had received two commissions for restoration work at Hexham Abbey and at Tynemouth Priory, though neither scheme was carried out. In 1824 Dobson made a careful restoration of the ruinous north transept window at St. Nicholas's, Newcastle; here he made a measured drawing of the structure and rebuilt it in a manner closely approximating to its original form. However, the building which really established Dobson's reputation as an ecclesiastical architect was the Anglican church of St. Thomas the Martyr, Newcastle (consecrated October 19th, 1830). It was built on a new and more populous site at the Barras Bridge, partly by the Corporation and partly by subscription, to replace the medieval chapel of St. Thomas's Hospital which was being demolished to widen the entrance from the old Tyne Bridge; it is a church remarkably characteristic of its time.

As towns and cities expanded during the first half of the 19th century an unprecedented number of churches and chapels were built to serve their needs. Successive governments, anxious to promote social stability after the Napoleonic Wars, encouraged this with subsidies for the building of Anglican churches. Acts of Parliament during the 1820s removed restrictions on Nonconformist sects, and the Catholic Emancipation Act of 1829 encouraged Roman Catholics to build their own churches too. The Nonconformists tended to favour classical architecture, the Roman Catholics ultimately Gothic. St. Thomas's is an early example in the North of England of neo-Gothic design and as such has been said to show 'the timidity with which architects then ventured upon the English mediaeval style'[4]. What it does reflect is the situation in the 1820s when, despite the growing interest in Gothic and medieval forms, there was still no clearly accepted style for Anglican church design. None was indicated on aesthetic grounds by the Commissioners appointed by Act of Parliament in 1818 to administer a church building grant of one million pounds, although for reasons of economy most of the churches built under their auspices were in the Gothic style. Leading architects of the day were invited by the Commissioners to suggest the most spacious and economical means of church design. Sir John Soane, for example, proposed three alternative types: Norman, Classical and Gothic. All took the form of a rectangular box with large windows, clearly on the Georgian or 'auditory' plan, and with steeple and entrance at the west; the Gothic version had buttresses and pinnacles of a rudimentary kind.

The design for St. Thomas's was selected from another trio of alternative schemes, submitted as models to the Committee of Newcastle Common Council on July 24th, 1827. The choice consisted of the preferred design, another by Dobson himself, and a third by the respected local architect John Green. The form of the latter two is not known, but may well have been classical; Dobson at least would have been unlikely to offer a second Gothic scheme. The design as executed was meant to be in 'the Gothic style of the thirteenth century'[5], or Early English, and while far from authentic represents a considerable advance on the kind of 'Commissioners' Gothic' proposed by Soane. Although not funded by the Commissioners, St. Thomas's does resemble their more convincing churches of that time, such as St. Peter's, Brighton (1824-28) by Charles Barry or J. Potter's Church of St. Mary, Sheffield (1826-29); all have a large centrally placed tower forming the western entrance to the church, and square rather Georgian proportions offset by a profusion of buttresses and pinnacles more decorative than structural in effect. St. Thomas's has more individuality than its counterparts through Dobson's determined, if idiosyncratic use of the Early English style, and there is no certainty that he was aware of these other designs. However, he may have been influenced by Rickman, who also admired Early English and specifically recommended the kind of coupled lancets, much increased in height[6], employed in this design.

Similar in style was Dobson's re-building of Belford Parish Church, Northumberland (1826-29) where to a basically Norman chancel he added a nave which has buttresses dividing lofty coupled lancets on the south, but with a tower of less distinctive form. An early but much more convincing exercise in Early English is St. Cuthbert's, Greenhead (1826), a small rectangular chapel (the chancel was added in 1900) beautifully sited, and built of local stone. Its single lancets are narrow and more archaeologically correct, and the design has the simplicity of genuine mediaeval work. Dobson, we are told, made a particular study of Early English forms[7] and in this case was surely inspired by local examples such as Lanercost Priory and Haltwhistle Parish Church.

St. Thomas's, meanwhile, is a transitional design retaining much of the character of the Georgian auditorium type of church which emphasised the congregation's convenience in following the service, with the pulpit as the focal point. Thus the

59

58. St. Cuthbert's, Greenhead, Northumberland, 1826

59. St. Thomas's, Newcastle upon Tyne, 1827—30. The interior

interior has an almost eighteenth century elegance. There is some sense of a nave with side aisles, but instead of division by arcades slender columns culminate in delicate stone vaults which seem to emphasise the fact that the aisles are almost as high as the nave. There is no chancel (though Dobson is said to have desired one)[8] and the altar occupies a small recess, while the architect must have regretted the addition of galleries in 1837 which block the windows and detract from the unusually light and spacious effect he first achieved. At Belford and Greenhead the galleries, which he did design, are positioned unobtrusively at the west. St. Thomas's was Evangelical in tone and even had a three decker pulpit (clerk's desk, reading desk, and pulpit) which Dobson is supposed to have disliked[9] but which, with galleries, was typical of Anglican church arrangements at the time.

Equally typical was Dobson's next major church, that of St. James, Benwell, of 1831-32. It has been much altered and enlarged, but plans survive indicating a rectangular scheme without aisles or chancel and with a centrally placed tower (without spire) providing the western entrance to the church. Inside there were galleries at the west and extending to the fourth bay of the nave on the north and south sides. The ground floor was totally occupied by seating, with pews surrounding even the clerk's desk, reading desk and pulpit — placed well to the west — from which services were conducted. A small altar table was situated directly below the triple windows at the east.

This design, however Georgian in plan, was quasi-medieval in effect: here Dobson uses for the first time, albeit tentatively, the neo-Norman mode. St. James's had undecorated arches and with its pediments was still rather classical in feel, but Dobson had already been employed to make surveys of Norman architecture at the Castle Keep[10] and St. Andrew's Church, Newcastle, and, despite the incompatibility of his work at Belford church, was to develop a substantial interest in the style. St. Cuthbert's, Bensham, (1845) is a similar but more advanced design, inspired by the 12th century church at Barfreston, Kent, which Dobson examined in 1844[11]. St. Cuthbert's has a five bay nave, like the Benwell church, but with a substantial apse, reflecting changes in liturgical ideas; a 'transitional' tower (with spire) at the south west, gives scope for the west wall to have triple windows under a single arch. Although an aisle was added in 1875, the effect inside is still simple and well proportioned, with shafts rising between the side windows to support the timbers of the roof; the finely carved 'chancel' arch appears to derive from the church of St. Andrew, Newcastle, which Dobson had restored in 1844, adding a south transept in similar neo-Norman style.

From about 1830 to 1860, during which time the greater part of Dobson's ecclesiastical work was done, the Gothic Revival developed from a trickle to a flood. It received a tremendous boost through the architecture and writings of Augustus Welby Northmore Pugin (1812-52), a Catholic convert who epitomised a yearning for the Middle Ages born of a desire for religion and a dissatisfaction with the urban and industrial chaos of modern times. He argued that the Protestant Reformation was responsible for a multitude of social ills which could be cured only by a return to medieval concepts of society and design. Gothic, being Christian, truthful and English, was the only style capable of symbolising religious ideas and in a Christian society the only architecture suitable for the whole range of purposes and forms.

As the Victorian period progressed thousands of churches were built; they were funded, often with difficulty, through a combination of private patronage, public subscription, and grants from organisations like the Incorporated Church Building Society and the Ecclesiastical Commissioners (convened in 1835). Within the Anglican world, Gothic became the accepted style of design. During the 1830s and 40s a popular alternative was neo-Norman, which even Pugin sometimes used, and as we have seen, St. James's, Benwell, was an early example of this form. But soon the national debate became not whether, but what form of Gothic should be employed.

The preference for Gothic went hand in hand with the Oxford, or 'Tractarian', Movement which sought to reform the Church of England by insisting upon the full importance of the Sacraments. It stressed the 'Catholic' tradition of the Church and wished to create a more spiritual outlook through the re-introduction of colour, ritual and symbolism. The 'Ecclesiologists' gave architectural expression to all this. In 1839 a group of High Church inclined undergraduates had formed the Cambridge Camden Society (later re-named the Ecclesiological Society) ostensibly as an antiquarian group, but with the real purpose of promoting clear and definite principles for church architecture. This, needless to say, had to be Gothic. Soon they had hundreds of well connected members, particularly clergymen, and exerted an immense influence through publication of numerous advisory tracts, and their magazine *The Ecclesiologist* from 1841. Their instructions and 'rules', persuasive in their

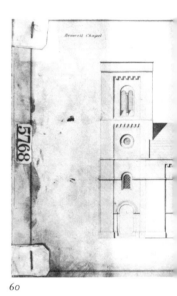

60

60. St. James's, Benwell, Newcastle upon Tyne, 1831—2. From a drawing by Dobson (RIBA)

61. St. Cuthbert's, Bensham, Gateshead, 1845

62. The Vicarage, Embleton, Northumberland, 1828

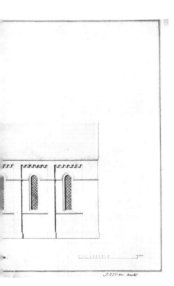

61

62

63

dogmatism, sought to re-introduce ritual and, in effect, adapt the ideas of Pugin to the context of Anglican worship and design. At first they tolerated Early English but before long fixed upon the 'Middle Pointed', their term for Early Decorated, as the only acceptable style. Perpendicular, being 'debased', was utterly taboo. Meanwhile the famous critic John Ruskin (1819-1900) was also advocating 'the English earliest decorated'[12] as opposed to the Perpendicular, or late Gothic style, and had begun to evolve a more general theory of Gothic architecture involving concepts such as colour, nature and truth. Thus his *The Seven Lamps of Architecture* (1849) had an enormous influence during the High Victorian period and later, although upon Dobson at least Ruskin's more complex ideas seem to have had remarkably little effect.

The Ecclesiologists had firm views on church restoration, which they believed it was a Christian duty to undertake, its purpose being to produce a correct 'Middle Pointed', or at the very least homogeneous effect, even if this meant the destruction of ancient work. The original form of a building, as first conceived, should as far as possible be restored. Dobson was prepared to go further than many Ecclesiologists in applying this principle to Perpendicular work; thus in about 1852 he made a scholarly re-construction of the Percy Chapel, Tynemouth Priory, delighting in the sculptured bosses of its roof[13]. However, as early as 1817 Dobson had proposed to replace the late Gothic east window at Hexham Abbey with triple lancets which in his opinion were more in keeping with the building's basic form, and most of his later restorations, though conditioned by the individual preferences of clergymen and other patrons, were generally in accordance with orthodox Ecclesiological ideas. Thus at St. Michael's, Houghton-le-Spring, he re-built the nave roof to a pitch he thought it had once had. At Embleton church, Northumberland, he re-built the 'Craster' porch, removed the galleries, and extended the nave aisles westward as far as the west wall of the tower, incorporating the latter into the body of the church; in the lower portion of the tower he inserted a ceiling supported by stone arches, the springers of which were designed to rest in the spaces of some early Norman windows which Dobson had blocked up[14]. All other windows were re-built with 'Middle Pointed' tracery. The effect was to remove what one observer had affectionately described as 'the varied ornaments, excrescences and inconveniences'[15] contributed by different generations over the years. Incidentally, Dobson's work here can be contrasted with the thoroughly High Victorian chancel added only sixteen years later by F.R. Wilson in 1866-67, inspired by Ruskin with its bands of different coloured stone. When Dobson came to deal with St. Michael's, Ford, in 1852, this largely 13th century church consisted of a single aisled nave and chancel, the latter entered through a very narrow arch, and externally presented a picturesque appearance with various types of window and a large irregular 'transept' on the south. Dobson kept the unusual bell tower but otherwise swept all irregularity away, blocking up the west door, adding the north aisle and present south porch, and replacing the chancel arch. He re-roofed the nave,

64

raising its pitch by some eight feet. All the windows, except for an ancient lancet in the west wall, were re-constructed in a uniform Early English style. The result was to increase seating accommodation and to 'tidy up', in a manner desired by many clergymen at the time. There is no doubt that Dobson expressed his love of Gothic through this kind of work, and believed that he was engaged in the valuable task of preserving buildings for posterity. Yet the effect of these and many other restorations of that time was to produce structures that can be obtrusively 19th century in tone.

The Ecclesiologists also insisted on the proper incorporation of Christian symbolism into modern church design. Thus a church should be cruciform in shape, or at least make allusion to the Trinity through the use of triple windows or in its general form. It should have a proper altar, preferably of stone, and above all a clearly defined nave and chancel, divided by a chancel arch and screen. Galleries were absolutely forbidden.

Dobson is known to have admired some of Pugin's work[16], and seems to have been influenced by Ecclesiology, or at least by this general climate of ideas. Certainly most of his later churches are Gothic, and more authoritively so; some, such as St. John's, Otterburn, are quite Ecclesiologically 'correct'. He used the Decorated style more, and gradually abandoned the notion of symmetrical tower and facade. Also, while prefering Tudor for ancillary buildings such as vicarages and schools, for almshouses he could employ a domestic Gothic of which even Pugin would have approved. However, he continued to favour Early English and even, as we have seen, neo-Norman modes, and to the very end of his career could produce a thoroughly non-Ecclesiological church design. For example, St. Paul's, Elswick, (1857-59) has no proper chancel — for which it was criticised by the Incorporated Church Building Society — and nor has Jesmond Parish Church (1858-61); built in memory of the celebrated local pastor, Richard Clayton, the latter has longitudinal galleries as well, carefully placed between two tiers of aisle widows, the upper under gables which are at right angles to the axis of the nave. Inside, the galleries (so unusual for their date) flank a well proportioned nave with stately arcades, from the spandrels of which delicately carved stone shafts rise to support a splendid open timber roof. The five light east window, upon which lines of sight inexorably converge, is also particularly fine. This is a sturdy, vigorous church of unorthodox design, in a freely adapted Decorated style with considerable variety of window tracery and other forms. The west end, for example, has two large windows surmounted by a rose window and gable cross. The main body of the church — the polygonal vestry was added later by R.J. Johnson — has a roof of single pitch and the tower, unexpectedly placed at the south east, seems even more massive as a result of not being built to its intended height; it is pinnacled and at the upper level has pairs of windows on each side. The exterior of the church is heavily buttressed and much of the detail is finely carved. There are gargoyles and everywhere the hood mouldings terminate in expressively sculpted heads of prophets,

63. St. Mary's Hospital Almshouses, Newcastle upon Tyne, 1851

64. St. Paul's, Elswick, Newcastle upon Tyne, 1857—9

65

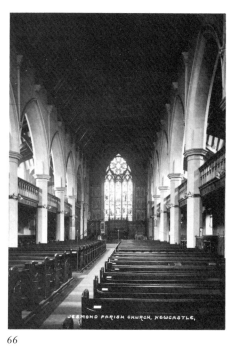

66

kings and saints. This feature occurs almost identically in other examples of Dobson's later ecclesiastical work such as the churches at Gilsland, Elswick and Ford, and suggests that while the architect is known to have used several different building firms, a specialist team of carvers may also have been recurrently employed.

Dobson did remove galleries at Embleton, Hexham and Houghton-le-Spring, but actually added them at Hartburn (1835) and at Bishopwearmouth church (1849-50). The Evangelical tradition died hard in the North, and Dobson was not doctrinaire; also, he was 'impartial' in serving all denominations, and in providing a wide variety of plans and types, responded to demand. His Nonconformist churches had galleries, as one might expect, but many of his later Anglican schemes, such as St. Cuthbert's, Bensham, and St. Peter's, Oxford Street, Newcastle, (1840-43) retained them at the west. St. Peter's had a western tower, centrally placed, and Dobson only incorporated a chancel after the vicar decided it might improve the original design[17]. Otherwise this church had considerable authenticity, being in a late Decorated style (admired by Sydney Smirke) with aisles and clerestory, and the internal effect was spacious with a substantial chancel arch. Unusually large and rich in form, it was a mature example of his work. Also 'Decorated' and surprisingly ornate was the Church of the Divine Unity, Newcastle, (1853). Its plan, however, reflected Nonconformist practice in being a simple rectangle with galleries, supported by slender iron columns, around three sides.

Dobson's urban churches of all denominations were usually built on a limited budget of between three and seven thousand pounds; this was probably a factor in the frequent choice of the simplest, Early English forms. He provided as many adaptations of the style as he could, with timber roofs, often with spirelets or simple bell towers, and groups of lancets at the east and west. A good example is All Saints', Monkwearmouth, (1846-49); this has a spirelet at the south west angle of the nave (combined with south aisle under a single roof), chancel and south porch. An excellent effect is achieved by simple means. Trinity Presbyterian Church, New Bridge Street, Newcastle, (1846) had twin towers at the west, between which was a group of seven lancets resembling those at St. Edmund's Chapel, Gateshead, which Dobson had restored (1836-37). St. Joseph's Roman Catholic church, Birtley, (1842) had five lancets at the west, with a modest spirelet above. Laygate Presbyterian church, South Shields, (1848-49) was paid for by the local industrialist J. Stevenson and thus had an impressive tower (in this case at the south west) with characteristic brooch spire, almost identical to that of a contemporary Dobson church, St. Cuthbert's, Shotley Bridge.

65. Jesmond Parish Church, Newcastle upon Tyne, 1858—61

66. Jesmond Parish Church, Newcastle upon Tyne, 1858—61. Interior

67. St. Peter's, Newcastle upon Tyne, 1840—3. Interior from an oil painting by J.W. Carmichael (Laing Art Gallery, Newcastle upon Tyne)

68. St. Peter's, Newcastle upon Tyne, 1840—3

69. Church of Divine Unity, Newcastle upon Tyne, 1853. From a lithograph (Laing Art Gallery, Newcastle upon Tyne)

67

68

69

Lack of money often hampered Dobson's work. Towers were sometimes not completed as designed, as at Jesmond Parish Church, and on some occasions he had to resort to expedients such as providing roofs of cheaper timber stained as oak. In the case of St. Paul's, Elswick, one of the largest churches he designed, Dobson complained that he had been unable to make the exterior more attractive through want of funds[18]. The church has nave, aisles and clerestory but the internal effect, though spacious, is extremely plain.

During the latter part of his career Dobson was even more involved in restoration work, but earlier Ecclesiological ideas on this were beginning to be attacked. In 1849 Ruskin stated that 'restoration' meant 'the most total destruction a building can suffer: a destruction out of which no remnants can be gathered: a destruction accompanied with false description of the thing destroyed'[19]. His reverence for old work, shared by his disciple William Morris, underlies a general attitude today that ancient architecture should be kept intact. Antiquarians, and even some of the later Ecclesiologists, began to be influenced by these views. In 1852, the Archaeological Institute of Great Britain held its annual meeting in Newcastle upon Tyne; when

72

70

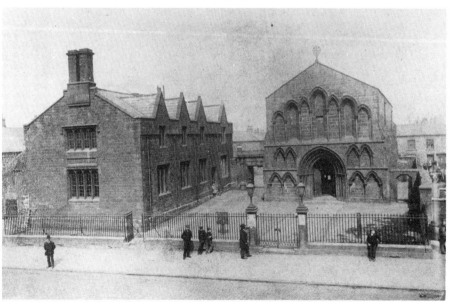

71

74

Dobson took members on a guided tour of the town, he found himself obliged to defend his reconstruction of the north transept window at St. Nicholas's Church, claiming that departures from its original form had been forced upon him by the churchwardens of the day. Seven years later he rebuilt the east gable of the same church, replacing the old Perpendicular window and circular light above, with the present enormous, semi-Perpendicular design. Taken to task by his fellows at the Society of Antiquaries, he managed to explain that at least he had successfully opposed the Church authorities' preference for an even less authentic Decorated scheme[20]. Even more controversial were Dobson's last major restorations, at Hexham Abbey and Kirknewton church. At Kirknewton he completely rebuilt the nave and north aisle in Early English style, but the distinguished architect Anthony Salvin, hitherto a friend and supporter of Dobson, vehemently opposed the plan[21]. He argued that it was structurally unnecessary and incompatible with existing elements such as the 12th century south chantry and tiny chancel, with their crude but unusual barrel vaults.

70. All Saints', Monkwearmouth, Durham, 1846—9

71. Holy Trinity Church, Gateshead, and the Ellison School, 1836—7

72. Presbyterian Church, South Shields, Durham, 1848. From an old photograph

73. Hexham Abbey, Northumberland. The east window of 1858

74. St. John's, Otterburn, Northumberland, 1855—7

75. St. Edward's, Sudbrooke Holme, Lincolnshire, 1860—2

73

75

Salvin feared the demolition of these 'incorrect' portions of the church, although ultimately they were spared. At Hexham in 1858 Dobson finally got the chance to remove the east window of the Abbey which he had examined in 1817 and been obliged to restore in 1828. Now he replaced this unusual late Gothic five light structure, with 'rose' as centrepiece, with two tiers of lancets based on those at Whitby Abbey which he deemed to be contemporary with the building's basic form. Also he completely removed the Perpendicular Lady Chapel below, though he had drawn up plans to restore this about seven years before. The effect today is hard, neat and academically correct, but was censured by the journals of the time in the severest terms.

In spite of the controversies of these last years, Dobson achieved great success with two new churches built by him, St. John's, Otterburn, (1855-57) and St. Edward's, Sudbrooke, Lincolnshire, (1860-62); these are probably his most attractive churches. Both were paid for by generous private funds, have rural sites, and are generally similar in plan. St. John's is a small church in the Decorated style, and St. Edward's is equally intimate in scale. The latter has enriched arches with nave, chancel and apse, and is freely based on the 12th century Steetly Chapel near Chesterfield; in paying this final homage to the neo-Norman mode Dobson seems to have drawn upon various other studies he had made at Lanercost Priory and at the little Northumberland church at Rock. In these very late designs Dobson produced a refinement, and delicacy of ornament, unprecedented in his work.

Notes

1 Obituary of Dobson in *The Building News*, 13 January 1865, pp.25—6.

2 Illustrated in *AA*, new series, vol. XV, facing p.196.

3 Dobson presented a copy of a treatise by Lewis Vulliamy to the Literary, Scientific and Mechanical Institution; see the *NCh*, 12 February 1825.

4 *The Building News, loc. cit.*

5 Reported in the *NC*, 28 July 1827.

6 T. Rickman, *op. cit.*, p.131.

7 *The Building News, loc. cit.*

8 Dobson, p.44.

9 *Ibid.*

10 See the drawings by Dobson illustrated in Mackenzie 1827, facing p.102.

11 See sketches based on a survey by Dobson in the RIBA Drawings Collection (Smirke collection Sketch Book vol. 5, pp.84—6).

12 J. Ruskin, *The Seven Lamps of Architecture*, 1849, chapter VII, section VII.

13 Dobson gave a paper on this subject to the Archaeological Institute of Great Britain in Newcastle, 26 August 1852.

14 Described by F.R. Wilson in *Proceedings of the Society of Antiquaries of Newcastle upon Tyne*, new series, vol. 3, p.176.

15 Archdeacon Singleton c. 1829, quoted in O. Craster, *A History of Embleton Parish Church*, p.5.

16 See a sketch attributed to Dobson of a church by Pugin at Warwick Bridge, Cumbria, in the RIBA Drawings Collection (Smirke collection Sketch Book vol. 5, p.91).

17 See correspondence in Lambeth Palace Library (ICBS file no. 2459).

18 *Ibid.* (file no. 5050).

19 J. Ruskin, *op. cit.*, chapter VI, section XVIII.

20 See *AA*, new series, vol. IV, pp.152—153.

21 See correspondence in Lambeth Palace Library (ICBS file no. 5529).

I. Section of the proposed conservatory at Gibside, Durham. Dobson's drawing of 1814 (Durham County Record Office)

II. Lilburn Tower, Northumberland, 1828. From a watercolour by Dobson and J.W. Carmichael (Laing Art Gallery, Newcastle upon Tyne)

LONGITUDINAL SECTION for a PROJECTED CONSERVATORY at GIBSIDE HOUSE

Scale of Feet

I

II

VI *More Country Houses 1840-1862*

As we saw at the end of Chapter 3, by the end of the 1830s a reaction had set in against the castellated Gothic style, inspired by the more functional approach to architecture of the powerful propagandist A.W.N. Pugin. Similarly, though less suddenly, the Greek Revival style lost its appeal, and despite the popularity around the 1840s for Italianate styles which enabled classical details to be combined with picturesque plans and silhouettes, classical houses are rare in the Victorian period.

The overall tendancy in country house architecture was to what Robert Kerr, the author of the influential *The Gentleman's House*, called 'elegance and importance without ostentation'. Mostly this meant Elizabethan and Gothic styles which avoided symmetry and exploited tall gables, towers, and steep rooves.

As is clear from his ecclesiastical architecture, Dobson never fully accepted the new Victorian principles of design. Before 1840 his domestic architecture falls into two distinct categories, the plain, square, solidity of the Greek Revival, a style which later became intolerably old fashioned everywhere except Scotland; and the castellated Gothic which although increasingly unfashionable still had its adherents as late as the 1860s.

Dobson's undoubted emotional preference for the classical was allowed little opportunity for expression in his later years. Around 1840 he made some distinctly dull suggestions for classical additions to the interesting old house of Little Harle Tower in Northumberland[1]. Thomas Anderson had purchased the estate around 1835 after selling Anderson Place in Newcastle to Richard Grainger and wished to modernise and extend it. But Dobson's proposals are uninspired and totally unsympathetic to the older house. It is not surprising that they were rejected and that Anderson later designed his own idiosyncratic Gothic additions to the house, which have been recently demolished.

76. Lambton Castle, Durham, additions of c.1862

77. Holeyn Hall, Northumberland, 1858

Dobson was able to make minor additions and alterations to classical houses such as Newton Hall near Wylam, where a quite sympathetic bay to the south front and new staircase window etc. of 1851 develop the tripartite widow motif familiar from his work of the 1830s. At Holeyn Hall also near Wylam in 1858 he made substantial additions of a tower tied to the earlier 18th century house with heavy window surrounds and an elaborate balustrade.

At Wallington Hall Dobson was given an opportunity to work with one of the most beautiful 18th century houses in Northumberland[2]. In most respects it was work typical of those earlier in his career when he had been asked to improve the comfort of older houses, but at Wallington we have the additional dimension of the Pre-Raphaelite connections of the Trevelyans. Sir Walter Trevelyan inherited Wallington from his father in 1846 and to his friends' amazement chose to live in 'the large modern mansion' rather than his Elizabethan house of Nettlecombe in Somerset. But even to the Trevelyans, who seem to have despised modern comforts, the open courtyard of the house was unpleasantly dark, damp and cold.

Dobson was presumably chosen in 1852 to convert the courtyard into useable living space because of his years of experience with the houses of the Trevelyans' neighbours. His design was in a subdued Italianate style thoroughly appropriate to the rest of the house, though the hall impinges little on the older rooms with their exceptionally fine mid 18th century plasterwork. Only the staircase had to be rebuilt to accommodate the hall which rises, an independent structure, in two tiers of arcades towards a coffered ceiling. The designs had to be shown to John Ruskin for his approval, as Ruskin had become Pauline Trevelyan's mentor in all things artistic. Ruskin's only suggestion was that the conventional design of the balustrade around the upper gallery be replaced by one from Murano illustrated by Ruskin in his *The Stones of Venice*, volume II (just published). Dobson's architecture soon became the frame for a remarkable scheme of Pre-Raphaelite decoration by William Bell Scott, Master of the Government School of Design at Newcastle since 1843, Pauline Trevelyan and her friends, and John Ruskin himself. Of the eight large canvases of scenes from Northumbrian history which Scott painted in 1856-60 to fill eight blank ground floor arcades one, *Iron and Coal on Tyneside in the 19th century*, is an acknowledged Pe-Raphaelite masterpiece. Scott was keen that Dobson should not interfere with the proposed decorations.

In the bulk of his remaining work in the 1840s and 1850s Dobson adapts his Gothic skills and experience to the new climate of the early Victorian period. Angerton Hall, a house he repaired in the late 1820s was rebuilt in 1842 in a remarkably unfussy Tudor style with plain gables, unemphatic battlements, and tall windows on flat expanses of wall. The substantial service wing has recently been severely curtailed. The almost elegant simplicity of the design is a startling contrast with the houses of only five years previously such as Beaufront and Holme Eden. The difference may be partly one of cost, for the Gothic style was necessarily expensive, but it also reflects a change in architectural fashion within the period.

78. Wallington Hall, Northumberland. The hall, 1853

79. Angerton Hall, Northumberland, 1842

79

Sandhoe House of the following year is a more elaborate essay in the same manner though with Jacobean details, spikey pinnacles on the corners and gables and a delightful porch with scrolly gable and little Jacobean arcades with details that in their debased classical form a Georgian architect would not have tolerated. Inside, a heavy 17th century style stone fireplace in the hall may be original; a more conventional fireplace with its original grate is in the dining room. Both Angerton and Sandhoe are built of attractive stone in Dobson's favourite situation, over a south facing terrace.

The simplified Tudor style of Angerton was particularly appropriate for vicarages, an area in which Dobson was very active, at least eight being built between 1840 and 1855. Commissions for vicarages would arise naturally from Dobson's employment to build or restore a church or the house of the local landowner. Often church, vicarage and school would be built as a group of related buildings, as at Birtley for the Roman Catholic congregation. Dobson's vicarages are unexceptional and quite typical of the period, their Tudor elements being confined to mullioned windows, gables with prominent 'kneelers' and tall chimneys.

Among the larger houses of the period were the substantial additions made to Sudbrooke Holme in Lincolnshire built in a Tudor-Gothic style for Colonel Richard Ellison in 1851, but now demolished, and several houses around Hexham including The Hags, now Hackwood House, of 1843, and The Leazes of 1853. These last two confirm the increasing simplicity and informality of Dobson's Tudor style in this period, but they are small houses for modest clients.

A more ambitious house is Inglethorpe Hall near Wisbech in Norfolk built for Charles Metcalf, a Wisbech worthy, in 1857. This is a house that at once takes Dobson into the heart of High Victorian country house design. Here simplicity and informality are applied to a much larger composition, with many gables of different sizes, some partly crow-stepped. Perhaps uniquely for Dobson there is a steep roof over the staircase tower; the roof line is high and decorated, topped with a weathervane. The whole emphasis of the design is a vertical one, quite unlike the horizontal nature of early 19th century Gothic. The locality of the house demanded red brick, of a pleasantly varied hue, instead of the stone that Dobson would instinctively have preferred. But this material only adds to the modernity of the house, as brick was increasingly preferred by Victorian Gothic architects not only for economy but for its texture and colour.

80. Sandhoe House, Northumberland, 1843

81. Inglethorpe Hall, Norfolk, 1857

Inglethorpe seems to foresee George Gilbert Scott's desire, as expressed in *Remarks on Secular and Domestic Architecture* (1857), to create a Gothic domestic architecture of spacious and well-lit houses, with the most modern conveniences, uncluttered by archaic details, materials, and planning. The un-Dobsonian characteristics of the house suggest that Dobson, or his patron, had more advanced ideas in mind. At the time it was being designed Dobson had as a pupil E.R. Robson (from 1853-6) who was subsequently to become an assistant to Scott and then a pioneer of the 'Queen Anne' style of the 1870s and 1880s. But maybe the appearance of Inglethorpe is despite rather than because of this interesting connection.

It is more typical of Dobson that his last work, one of the most complex and ambitious of his life, should be a reversion to the stale conventions of castellated Gothic. Lambton Castle's restoration and enlargement took up the last 5 years of Dobson's working life. However, before looking at Lambton in more detail, a diversion must be made to Germany to note one of the more curious episodes in Dobson's life. Margaret Dobson refers to a request 'from a German nobleman... to design a crenellated mansion for him on the Rhine, (Dobson) went and saw the site and partly completed the plans but failing health compelled him to relinquish the task'[3]. Angus Fowler has recently identified the house as the Neues Schloss at Friedelhausen on the river Lahn (a tributary of the Rhine), built between 1852-4 for Adalbeit Baron von Nordeck zur Rabenau[4]. Dobson had probably met the Baron's English wife, Clara Phillips, in London around 1851 through her guardian's interest in railways. At any rate we know that Dobson was working on designs for the newly married couple's house in 1852 although they were never completed and the final form of the 'castelled mansion' was at least partially determined by the Baron's German architect, who did have, however, the benefit of several books on English Gothic and Tudor architecture.

83

The resulting building, on a prominent site facing west over the Lahr is a solid and dull rectangular block with tall octagonal corner turrets, with superficial similarities to some of Dobson's designs. However the design makes no attempt to create a picturesque silhouette and exploit the castle's romantic situation. The closest parallel to a design by Dobson is a previously unidentified drawing[5] of a heavily castellated house whose symmetry, large turrets, heavy machiolations, *porte-cochère*, and courtyard fountain are shared by the Neues Schloss. The German castle's entrance front is virtually a condensed version of this, surely earlier, design.

The rescue of Lambton Castle from mining subsidence and its subsequent massive enlargement is perhaps more notable as an engineering feat than as a contribution to architectural history[6]. The house has a long and complex history. Originally called Harraton Hall, the earlier 18th century house was rebuilt by Joseph Bonomi around 1800. The young John Lambton, later 1st Earl of Durham, then employed Ignatius Bonomi, Dobson's Durham contemporary and friend, to transform Harraton into a picturesque Gothic castle suited to its superbly romantic spot above an enormous terrace overlooking the River Wear. Bonomi's work, which took place between 1815 and 1828, included the landscaping of the park, bridges, lodge gates and walks as well as the great house itself.

However, Lambton had been built over old coal workings which, drained of water by subsequent mining operations, led in 1854 to the most destructive subsidence under Bonomi's west block. It is perhaps the ultimate compliment to Dobson's talents as an engineer that he should have been called in by the 2nd Earl in 1857 at the age of 69 to underpin the Castle and to design major new extensions to the Castle. Dobson worked with one of Lambton's coal-viewers, Mr. Heccles, to fill the empty coal seams (69 fathoms beneath the ground) with brickwork, and rebuild the foundations with 10 foot wide and 8 foot deep beds of concrete beneath the walls. Most of Bonomi's west

82. Design for a castellated mansion. From a drawing by Dobson (Laing Art Gallery, Newcastle upon Tyne)

83. Neues Schloss, Friedelhausen, Germany, 1852—4

block was pulled down and Dobson designed new reception rooms around a Great Hall. In style and plan they followed closely Bonomi's work of forty years earlier (except for the replacement of large Gothic windows with square headed ones), the result of deference to Bonomi's work but also of Dobson's innate stylistic conservatism.

The Great Hall was the most significant addition, but this was essentially a creation of Sydney Smirke who took over the work following Dobson's incapacitating stroke of 1862. Smirke was Dobson's son-in-law, having married Isabella Dobson in 1840. Dobson and Smirke's joint additions were largely demolished in the 1930s and Dobson's contribution to the house as it now remains is minimal.

Notes

1 Drawings in NCRO (660/18).
2 Raleigh Trevelyan, *A Pre-Raphaelite Circle*, 1978, pp.67—8, 78, 120.
3 Dobson, p.34.
4 Private communication, for which we are deeply grateful.
5 In the Laing Art Gallery, Newcastle upon Tyne.
6 *CL*, 24, 31 March 1966; perspective drawing in the Laing Art Gallery.

84. Lambton Castle, Durham. The additions of 1862 onwards by Dobson and Sydney Smirke

VII Building for Industry and Railways

The boundary between works of civil engineering and works of architecture is not clear cut, though it was clearer in the 19th century than it is today. Throughout the last century architecture was more often seen as the application of decoration to structure, rather than as the exploitation of the aesthetic merits of unadorned construction. Today works of engineering, such as bridges, warehouses, docks and piers are better appreciated for their 'architectural' qualities of elegance, proportion and efficient use of materials.

Although Dobson's architectural practice reached a climax with the designs for Newcastle's Central Station, in which engineering invention was matched by architectural ambition, it cannot be said that industrial architecture comprised a major part of his work. Engineering and constructional skills were of course vital, particularly to the larger works of public architecture, the prisons for example, and to his triumphant underpinning of Lambton Castle at the very end of his career, but there are relatively few surviving works of civil engineering through which we can analyse his approach to such work.

Docks and their associated buildings, obviously essential ingredients in the establishment of the North East as a major industrial and mercantile centre, are scattered through Dobson's career from the earliest years. He built two sets of docks at North Shields for local men in 1813 and 1816, planned improvements and extensions to the Quayside at Newcastle in 1836, 1848 and 1854, rebuilt the fishing harbour at Cullercoats in 1846 and designed staithes for Walker, Parker & Co., at the Elswick Lead Works. In the 1840 Newcastle Exhibition of Arts, Manufactures and Practical Science, he even exhibited a 'Working model of a Coal Drop, for lowering Waggons loaded with Coals to the Deck of the Vessel receiving them, — the weights returning the waggon when emptied, to the level of the railway'[1]. An enormous tobacco warehouse which narrowly escaped the great 1854 Quayside Fire, was built for Benjamin Sorsbie in 1818-19, the scale of which is illustrated by Dobson's advertisement for 220,000 bricks and 445 dozen flagstones[2]. An even larger warehouse was designed for the Newcastle, Berwick and North Shields Railway in 1847-50 on the present site of Manors Station, another railway warehouse at North Shields station in 1848, and in 1856-8, the only survivor, the Grain Warehouse at Hudson's South Dock in Sunderland. Strangely asymmetrical, with a large elliptical-arched bay off-centre, the warehouse is of brick with internal floors of timber supported on iron columns, by then a rather old fashioned constructional technique, but the design has a distinctive architectural quality,with a tall ground floor with round arched openings, four lower floors above with segmental-headed windows, the whole topped with a dentil cornice. The design was strong enough to have been imitated by Thomas Meik in 1859 for his adjoining warehouse. However both, at the time of writing, are due for demolition.

Manufacturing industry did not play a prominent part in Dobson's career; supposed work for the Cooksons at their South Shields glassworks has not been proved, but he did build a cornmill for R.S. Surtees at Hamsterley as early as 1819, a large coach factory in Pilgrim Street, Newcastle, for the important coach-builders, Messrs. Atkinson and Philipson, in 1837, for which he apparently also designed the machinery, and a substantial flax mill with bold classical detailing on the Ouseburn for Mr. Plummer in 1848. These are a seemingly random group, but it is significant that Dobson had worked for Surtees previously at Hamsterley Hall itself, and had designed Plummer's house at Gateshead Fell in 1823, so in those two instances it was a case of satisfied clients of Dobson's domestic work returning to him for designs of a different nature.

Dobson also designed a Gothic bridge for Surtees at Hamsterley in 1825, the first of several modest road bridges built at a time of major improvements to the country's road system. The state of Britain's roads in the 18th and early 19th centuries was recognised as a national scandal, and was a factor in encouraging the growth of the railways. Thomas Telford and J.L. McAdam were responsible for the major improvements in road construction in the 1810s and 1820s. Telford, also one of the

85. The Central Station, Newcastle upon Tyne, 1847—50. The roof

country's greatest bridge engineers, worked with Dobson on the new bridge over the Wansbeck at Morpeth, on the main Newcastle-Edinburgh road. 'Telford chose or approved of the site', Hodgson wrote, 'the designs... are by Mr. Dobson.'[3] It was built between 1829 and 1831 to replace the narrow medieval bridge which later fell into complete ruin. Dobson's other bridges, on the Mitford Road at High and Low Ford, at Chatton and Haltwhistle for example, included some wooden ones and were less important than that at Morpeth.

More significant than any of these road bridges, however, was a proposal Dobson made in 1843 for a High Level Bridge at Newcastle[4]. There were at least 15 proposals for High Level Bridges in the 19th century, some to take road or rail traffic alone, the more percipient to combine the two. Dobson provided three alternative designs, a 40ft. wide rail and foot bridge, a 60ft. wide bridge with rail and road on the same level, and a bridge with a road carried beneath the railway. It was to be an iron bridge carried on four arches over the river and one over the Close, sited rather to the west of the present bridge, in order to benefit from the anticipated growth of industry and residential development in Elswick. The Newcastle and Carlisle Railway Company, for whom Dobson made the designs, had purchased land west of Forth Banks where they hoped to provide a station for the joint use of their own line, the Newcastle and Darlington Junction Railway and a proposed Newcastle to Edinburgh railway. A surviving sketch by Dobson for a railway station for the Newcastle and Carlisle Railway presumably relates to this proposal[5]. The large Tudor Gothic design is a stretched out version of his country house designs of the 1830s, such as Beaufront and Holme Eden.

The original Carlisle terminus was a very modest Tudor station on London Road, built possibly to Dobson's design in 1836, but in 1837 the line was extended 1 mile to the north west and from 1863 the Newcastle trains shared the main line Citadel Station of 1848-51, designed by Sir William Tite.

There were several competing routes for the Edinburgh line. Dobson himself, in partnership with Matthias Dunn and the engineer Robert Hawthorn, had in 1836 drawn up a prospectus for a Newcastle to Dunbar railway[6], roughly on the present route, to be carried over the Tweed on another high level bridge at Berwick. George Stephenson had at the time preferred this coastal route of Dobson's to the inland alternatives, but when it came to the siting of the High Level Bridge at Newcastle he considered Dobson's location to be too far west and gave his approval to a rival proposal put forward by George Hudson and the bridge engineers and architects John and Benjamin Green on the site of the present bridge.

George Hudson's support was essential for any successful railway development in the North East in the 1840s, for he was single-mindedly devoted to creating a railway route under his control from London to Edinburgh. By 1845 Hudson was at the height of his powers and had become Chairman of the York and North Midland Railway, the Newcastle and Darlington Junction Railway, and the Newcastle and Berwick Railway, the last the successful inheritor of Dobson's 1836 proposal. Hudson was in control of all sections of the route, except the link across the Tyne. In 1844, he built a terminus station at Gateshead to designs by G.T. Andrews and in that year trains first ran from London to the Tyne. In 1845 his economic power persuaded the Newcastle and Carlisle Railway to share with him a joint station at his preferred site, south of Neville Street in Newcastle, and in the same year Acts of Parliament were obtained allowing him to build the High Level Bridge and Newcastle Central Station. The Greens' design for the bridge was abandoned in favour of one by George Stephenson detailed by Thomas Harrison, and Dobson was commissioned to design the Central Station.

Suggestions that Dobson was involved in the designs for the High Level Bridge seem to be unfounded though he may have contributed to the detailing of some of the approach viaducts, such as that over Dean Street. Certainly he was paid £490 by the Newcastle and Darlington Junction Railway for the 'High Level Bridge' work, but this may have been for his work in valuing the property to be demolished, whereby 800 families lost their homes[7].

Hudson's power and ambition grew. In 1845 he was also elected M.P. for Sunderland in place of Lord Howick, an opponent of his Northumberland East Coast line and recently elevated to Earl Grey. He invested heavily on behalf of the Newcastle and Darlington Junction Railway in the Sunderland Dock Company, for which Dobson was later to build the Grain Warehouse; in 1847 he decided to develop Whitby as a fashionable watering place in order to increase traffic on the Whitby branch of his York and North Midland Railway. To this end he set up the Whitby Building Company which acquired fields on West Cliff and began to build crescents and terraces to Dobson's plans (see p.88).

86. Grain warehouses, South Dock, Sunderland. The left by Dobson 1856—8, the right by T. Meik, 1859 (Sunderland Museum and Art Gallery)

87. Messrs. Atkinson and Philipson's Coach Manufactory, Newcastle upon Tyne, 1837. From an engraving (Laing Art Gallery, Newcastle upon Tyne)

88. Morpeth Bridge, Northumberland, 1829—31

ATKINSON & PHILIPSONS

87

86

RESS ESTABLISHMENT.

88

On 31st December 1848 Hudson's two companies, the York, Newcastle and Berwick Railway (which by then had acquired the Newcastle and Carlisle Railway) and the Newcastle and Darlington Junction Railway, declared unexpectedly low dividends. At the next shareholders' meeting questions began to be asked about the financial management of the companies, about Hudson's part in share dealings within and between his companies and about his personal financial relationship with them. As details of various illegal activities were uncovered during the subsequent investigations, the shares of the companies collapsed in price and the years of 'Railway Mania' came to a sudden end. Hudson resigned his chairmanship during the year, but continued to be popular and widely admired for his achievements; he remained Sunderland's M.P., for example, until 1859.

The architectural result of this sudden collapse in public confidence and in the financial powers of the companies was that Dobson's magnificent first design for the Central Station was not carried out, and when the building was eventually completed it was but a ghost of his original conception.

Dobson's design of c.1848 was of great nobility; two parallel *porte-cochères* lay behind 34 pairs of grand Roman Doric columns flanking arched openings on a tall plinth. The great central portico carried giant seated figures. The use of arches and the Roman order is symptomatic of the move in the 1840s from Greek classicism, with its plain walls and strictly rectangular openings, to Roman and Italianate styles, with their rusticated walls, round-headed windows and arches. Roman classicism was grander, more decorated, more extravagant and carried overtones of luxury and imperial spendour, rather than the intellectual rigour and discipline of the Greek. In the 1840s Greek Revival buildings began to be characterised as 'insipid' and Victorian Imperialism sought its expression in the style of Imperial Rome, flavoured with a wider appreciation of Continental, particularly French, classical styles. Self-confidence, a notable quality in Victorian architecture, and in intellectual and technological thought generally, is also evident in Dobson's design, in what was the most splendid expression of the supreme confidence of the men who built Britain's railways. If the design had been built it would have undoubtedly have produced the finest railway station outside London.

The design of a railway station facade is crucially dependent on whether the facade lies alongside the tracks, as at Newcastle, or, as in the case of a terminus station like King's Cross in London, is at right angles to the tracks. In the latter instance, as Lewis Cubitt's station so superbly demonstrates, the opportunity for the facade to reflect the internal forms of the great curved iron and glass train sheds can give rise to an expressive nobility.

Dobson's facade, 590 feet long, gives no hint of the subtle glories of the train shed behind, which like Newcastle's Grey Street, makes superb use of the gentle curve on which it lies. No other station, except perhaps Thomas Prosser's rather later York Station of 1877, achieves so much from the combination of large scale, fine detailing in iron, glass and stone, and the interacting curves of the tracks and the roof members. Fortunately, much of this is still visible today through careful retention of the structure and lack of clutter on the platforms.

90

89

89. Proposed railway station for the
Newcastle and Carlisle Railway, c.1840. From
a drawing by Dobson (RIBA)

90. The Central Station, Newcastle upon
Tyne. The original design of c.1848 from a
watercolour by Dobson and J.W. Carmichael
(Laing Art Gallery, Newcastle upon Tyne)

91. The Central Station, Newcastle upon
Tyne, 1848—50. The interior, from a
watercolour by Dobson and J.W. Carmichael
(Laing Art Gallery, Newcastle upon Tyne)

91

92

The use of curved iron principals for the roof was as Dobson noted 'a new style of roofing'[8] and was achieved by rolling the iron out between bevelled rollers. This saved the expense of cutting the iron out of flat plates of iron; a virtue illustrative of Dobson's practical approach to engineering and constructional matters. The ironwork was by Hawks, Crawshay and Company of Gateshead; the innovation won Dobson a Gold Medal at the 1858 Paris Exposition.

The station's costs and facilities were to be shared between the Newcastle and Carlisle Railway and the York, Newcastle and Berwick Railway. Each had separate platforms, offices and staff. It was begun in 1846 and opened by Queen Victoria and Prince Albert on 29th August 1850; their busts by David Dunbar the younger still sit inside the entrance to the station. But Dobson must have been greatly disappointed. However fine his train shed was, the Neville Street frontage of the station was a sad testimony to the financial crisis that had hit the railways (the disgraced figure of George Hudson was not present, or indeed mentioned, during the opening speeches). The wings of the station facade lacked their *porte-cochères* which had had to be abandoned for economy and to accommodate a change in plan necessitated by the provision of a suite of offices for staff transferred from York to Newcastle. The central portico, which in Dobson's last attenuated design still survived to echo the Roman grandeur of his original scheme, was still unbuilt. It was not until 1863 that Dobson and Thomas Prosser, then architect to the North Eastern Railway, designed and built a simplified version of the original portico, which does at least have the scale and dignity of the earlier design.

As built, the corner pavilions at the extremities of the wings are in fact rewarding compositions, reminiscent of the corners of Wren's St. Paul's Cathedral, betraying French and English baroque influence. The wings between these pavilions and the portico are, however, unsatisfactory designs, unhappily marrying bold semicircular windows on the first floor with pairs of narrow rectangular windows beneath, separated by rather flat and wide entablature and pilasters. They tell of compromise and last-minute changes.

Despite, or perhaps because of these setbacks, Dobson continued to exhibit models and drawings of his first and finest designs at the Great Exhibition in London in 1851

92. The Central Station, Newcastle upon Tyne. The final design of c.1849—50, from a drawing by Dobson and J.W. Carmichael (Laing Art Gallery, Newcastle upon Tyne)

III. Beaufront Castle, Northumberland, 1837. The billiard room, from a watercolour by Dobson and J.W. Carmichael (Laing Art Gallery, Newcastle upon Tyne)

IV. The Royal Arcade, Newcastle upon Tyne, 1831—2. From a watercolour by Dobson and J. W. Carmichael (Laing Art Gallery, Newcastle upon Tyne)

III

IV

V

VI

V. The Green Market, Newcastle upon Tyne, 1834—5. From a watercolour by Dobson and J.W. Carmichael (Laing Art Gallery, Newcastle upon Tyne)

VI. St. Thomas's, Newcastle upon Tyne, 1827—30. From a watercolour by Dobson and J.W. Carmichael (Laing Art Gallery, Newcastle upon Tyne)

and at the Manchester Art Treasures Exhibition of 1857. Dobson hardly ever exhibited his designs outside Newcastle and seems to have made little effort to seek work outside the North of England. However, the wider exposure given to his Central Station designs contributed greatly to his reputation outside the region.

While the Central Station was building Dobson made two very much smaller station designs for the York, Newcastle and Berwick Railway, at Half Moon Lane in Gateshead and at Manors in Newcastle, both long since lost, and a very large warehouse at Manors, built over a filled-in part of Pandon Dene 'which was at the time only town deposit, and of a depth of 50 to 60 feet, and that for the most part in a state of fermentation... the settlement [of the completed warehouse] not exceeding 7in. over the whole.'[9] Dobson was, rightly, as proud of his engineering skills as he was of his architectural designs.

Notes

1 Catalogue no. 'Music Room 42'.

2 *NCh*, 2 January 1819.

3 Hodgson, II 2, p.426.

4 R.W. Rennison, *The High Level Bridge, Newcastle; its erection, design and construction*, 1981 (typescript in Newcastle Central Library), pp.10—11.

5 RIBA Drawings Collection (G6/39).

6 W.W. Tomlinson, *The North Eastern Railway, Its Rise and Development*, 1915, p.292.

7 R.W. Rennison, *op. cit.*, p.27.

8 Wilkes, p.109.

9 Wilkes, p.110.

DOORWAY of the CASTLE, NEWCASTLE. 49.

VIII *Public Architecture 1840-1862*

In 1847 Dobson extensively restored the old castle of Newcastle upon Tyne, paying particular attention to the chapel and the entrance to the hall. The work was carried out under the auspices of the Society of Antiquaries for use as its Museum, the Corporation having granted money and a lease. The Society held a banquet in the great hall to celebrate its re-occupation of 'the grand old keep'[1], but accommodation soon became inadequate and in 1855 it accepted what now seems a rather dubious plan by Dobson, apparently shelved through lack of funds, to organise more exhibition space. This would have involved placing a new floor over the great hall, thus recreating an upper apartment which many believed to have existed before, and inserting a domed window in the roof above. By this time the Society was engaged in a successful campaign against the proposed destruction of the Black Gate, then a rabbit warren of slum dwellings, which the opening out of the roadway from the High Level Bridge had left exposed. The Corporation was persuaded to offer a prize for the design of a new street frontage involving an approach to the Black Gate, now separated by the railway from the Keep itself. The designs, never to be carried out, were exhibited at the Merchants' Court in 1856. There is a watercolour by Dobson which seems to relate to one of these and illustrates a remodelled Black Gate with gables and turrets galore, flanked by battlemented Gothic ranges with buttresses and blind arches within the bays. Clearly the architect had lost none of his determination to redesign the castle area, and another proposal by him of 1856, to convert the arches of the adjacent railway viaduct to Museum use, may also have been included in this extravagant scheme. The latter no doubt formed the basis of plans that Dobson submitted to the City Council in 1859 for 'the proposed Museum in connection with the castle, so framed as not to hide the keep or St. Nicholas' Church and also to bring in the Black Gate as part of a whole'[2]. Nothing however came of this, even when the Society later acquired the Black Gate.

Dobson's major public work of this period was a substantial addition to the old Newcastle Infirmary at the Forth which had become overcrowded and totally unequal

93. The restored entrance to the Castle Keep, Newcastle upon Tyne, 1847

94. The Black Gate Museum extension. An unexecuted proposal by Dobson of 1856, from a watercolour by Dobson (Private Collection)

94

to its task. The extension was built at a cost of £10,500, largely through subscriptions and donations, and consisted of a three storey wing, with basement containing services, dispensary and an outpatients' department; it was sited at right angles to an earlier extension of 1801-03, giving the maximum ventilation, space and light. Externally it matched the existing blocks, being a simple classical structure of utilitarian form. The Infirmary's centenary in 1851 had led its Committee to decide on a scheme of enlargement incorporating the most modern developments in hospital design, encouraged by their patron the Duke of Northumberland and by their senior surgeons, T.M.Greenhow and C.J.Gibbs[3]. Dobson was given the commission virtually as a matter of course and became a member of a Building Committee which inspected hospitals in Manchester, Liverpool, Birmingham and London during the summer of 1851. He even made a separate visit to a new hospital in Brussels and, with characteristic interest in the technical aspects of design, presented plans of all the hospitals visited to accompany the Committee's very thorough Report of 1852. Dobson and his colleagues particularly admired St. Thomas's Hospital, London, the newer parts of which typified the modern 'pavilion' system with large open wards (usually having nurses' rooms and w.c.'s at each end) rather than the old, small, subdivided type[4]. This was introduced in Dobson's Newcastle wing — together with the removal of partition walls from the existing wards — which was obliged to accommodate typhus and cholera patients even before completion in 1856. The operating theatre remained unchanged, however, and the infections which bedevilled hospitals of the time continually re-appeared until antiseptic surgery was generally introduced. The Infirmay was evacuated in 1906 and demolished in 1954.

By the 1850s one of Dobson's earlier public works had become a matter of serious concern. Despite, or perhaps because of, its 'advanced' design, the Newcastle Gaol had never been entirely satisfactory in use. With each floor of its radiating blocks accommodating only a single row of cells, it had become overcrowded due to an increase both in population and crime, and by 1856 had twice as many inmates as it was supposed to contain. A Government Inspector had recommended alterations as early as 1838, with the City Council agreeing in principle to enlargement in 1844. But nothing was done and throughout the 1840s and '50s official reports criticised the prison for its management and plan; it was referred to as 'ill adapted to its purpose' and 'a nursery of crime'[5]. Certain children had been confined in it fifty or sixty times. The main problem was that prisoners could not be separated from each other or kept under efficient control as a result of their mingling in the communal rooms. Nor could the gaol be enlarged beyond its walls owing to its constricted site, itself condemned as too easily communicating with the outside. Meanwhile, it is interesting to note that Morpeth prison had not only proved efficient, but more capable of expansion and being brought up to date.

In 1857 the Newcastle Council, having considered the possibility of a completely new gaol, agreed that the present situation was injurious to the prisoners and discreditable to the town, and decided to hold a competition 'for the best and most economical plan for remedying the existing ... defects'[6]. However, nothing came of this and, amid accusations of jobbery, Dobson was invited to submit plans and reports in 1857 and 1858. The ageing but indefatigable architect reminded the Gaol Committee, with much respect, of the omission of one of the radiating buildings originally proposed in 1822. He recommended at least one new building on what was now known as the 'separate system', rigorously separating classes of prisoner at all times; it was impossible, he said, to extend the prison eastwards at the back of Trafalgar Street. Initially he was prepared to demolish one or more of his radiating blocks. However, after visiting the principal prisons in England and conferring with prison governors he worked out a scheme with the help of Sir John Kincaid (the Senior Government Inspector) which would provide 225 more cells without interfering with the radiating blocks[7]. This was carried out between 1859 and 1861 at a cost of approximately £15,000; further additions became necessary later in the century and ultimately the prison was closed in 1925.

Although there is no evidence that Dobson canvassed for support, the complaint that Council Committees had too often favoured him with public works instead of organising competitions for designs, had been made before, as with his plan to redevelop the Newcastle Quayside. This had been necessitated by a disastrous explosion and fire in October 1854 which destroyed most of the Quayside's medieval 'chares' and in which, tragically, Dobson's promising son Alexander had been killed. At first the Council saw it as a good opportunity to improve a notoriously unhealthy area of the town, and almost immediately Dobson was asked to draw up plans. His detailed Report of November 1854 proposed improvements which he claimed to have

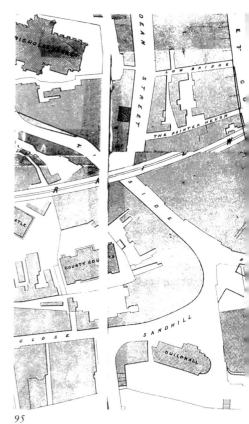

95

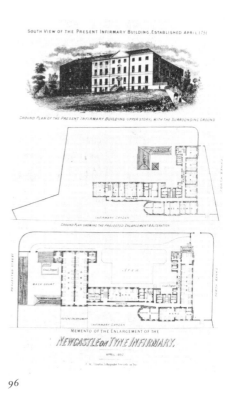

96

95. Plan of proposed new streets on the site of the Quayside fire, Newcastle upon Tyne, 1854. From a lithograph

had in mind for many years — a new street parallel to the Quayside from the Sandhill to Sandgate, with three lateral streets running to the Quay (part of which was to be glass roofed for the conduct of business and exchange) and a street linking Trafalgar Street with the Quay. The latter, he argued, would solve more effectively the longstanding problem of limited access between the upper and lower parts of town, especially now that the Manors Warehouse had been built, than the Council's idea of extending Pilgrim Street; however, he did include this possibility in his plan. He also advocated a street continuing the Side to Collingwood Street, passing under the intended High Level Bridge approach, thus providing a link between the Central Station and the Quay[8].

Dobson and his former pupil the Town Surveyor Robert Wallace were also employed to value the property involved, arriving at an estimate of £60,000. Dobson's plans were revised and re-revised but by May, 1856 had been accepted together with a design for street elevations, apparently selected from alternative schemes by him, which was praised for its variety, convenience for purchasers, cheapness, and for being 'in unison with the style of buildings in the old part of the town'[9]. A drawing by Dobson in the Laing Art Gallery must relate to this; it shows a Quayside development with an astonishing mixture of Tudor, Gothic and Renaissance facades, as though built over a period of several centuries, more or less to a common building line and height but sprouting a profusion of gables, turrets and crests. The formality of Dobson's earlier planning ideas could hardly be more at variance with this eclectic, if imaginative scheme, in which he was aiming for informality, to accord with the remaining medieval buildings of the old Quayside. Also, there might have been the influence of recent visits the architect had made to Belgium and probably Germany, where he is said to have admired the picturesque old towns[10].

Meanwhile, even by 1857 the Council had been completely unable to dispose of the sites, and, amid protests that the property had been overvalued and that an architectural competition should have been arranged, sold the entire area to the developer Ralph Walters at a bargain price. Walters, a native of Newcastle but then resident in London, turned to younger local architects like William Parnell to design

97

96. Plan of the proposed enlargement of the Infirmary, Newcastle upon Tyne, 1852. From an engraving

97. Proposed elevations of buildings on the site of the Quayside fire, Newcastle upon Tyne, c.1854. From a drawing by Dobson (Laing Art Gallery, Newcastle upon Tyne)

the spacious Italianate buildings of 1858-63 which we see today. The final scheme was conditioned less by Dobson's elevations than by his street plan, but even here his valuable proposals to link the Quayside with the upper town were not carried out.

Town planning was continuing to be an important element during the latter part of Dobson's career. Between 1851 and 1857 he laid out streets in the expanding part of Monkwearmouth between the Wear bridge and the docks, for the landowner Sir Hedworth Williamson[11], and as late as 1860 proposed a new street, possibly in the Gothic style, to continue his earlier St. Mary's Place, Newcastle. At Monkwearmouth, Dame Dorothy, Dock, Ann (later Victor), Barrington, Hardwicke, Bloomfield, Mulgrave and Normanby Streets and Millum Terrace were built in a conventional grid pattern on land which had formerly been a ballast hill; they consisted of neat, two storey brick terraces with basements (all now demolished) representing an unusually high quality of working class housing for the area at this time, in line with the developer's usual approach. It is probable, though not absolutely certain, that Dobson designed both houses and streets[12].

Much grander was his plan for the West Cliff development at Whitby (1857), undertaken for his old patron George Hudson, who had intended to expand his railway system and develop the town as a fashionable resort; it consists of classical terraces, rather like those at Tynemouth, facing the Abbey and the sea[13]. East Terrace and the Royal Crescent are particularly fine, the latter having dignified four storied houses with basements, and with rusticated ground floors, pedimented windows and balconies. Once again, however, Hudson's financial problems prevented full implementation of the scheme.

The stylistic plurality characteristic of Dobson's later work is nowhere more apparent that in his public buildings of the time. For example, his North Shields Town Hall, largely financed by a local benefactor Joseph Laing, is in a very informal Tudor style, with a double L-shaped plan turning the corner of Howard and Saville Streets and completing the section between Howard Street and Norfolk Street. It was built in two separate parts from 1844-45 which means that the battlemented ranges with decorative gables and, at one corner, an oriel window below a plainer gable, harmonise only reasonably well; however, the building was meant to cater for a variety of functions including that of a Mechanics' Institution (added in the second phase) and the emphasis is less on civic monumentality than on fitting in with the domestic scale of the street.

By contrast the Newcastle Riding School (1847) can be described as classical, but is a dour utilitarian structure, now long disused, which was clearly designed to do little more than fulfil its function of providing the maximum amount of space. Unusually

98

98. Royal Crescent, Whitby, North Yorkshire, 1857

99. Town Hall, North Shields, 1844—5

100. Barber-Surgeons' Hall, Newcastle upon Tyne, 1851

101. Gas Company Office, Newcastle upon Tyne, 1861—2. From a drawing by Dobson (Tyne and Wear Archives)

99

100

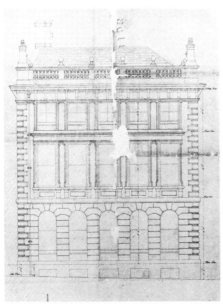

101

for a Dobson public building it is brick, but stone is used for some of its oversimplified details (quite unlike those of his Sunderland Warehouse, another utilitarian building) such as the surrounds of the three round arched windows on the street facade, looking towards the site of his earlier Northumberland Baths. Incidentally, for most of the second half of the 19th century the recruits at the Riding School received instruction from the famous Sergeant Major J. Burghersh Forbes, a hero of the 'Light Brigade'. Meanwhile, Dobson's Bricklayers' Hall, near the Castle Garth, was Gothic (1851), while his Northumberland Dock Office, North Shields, of 1859-61, part of the then general development of the River Tyne, is a block-like neoclassical design recalling his much earlier work. It is now derelict, though superbly built of stone; originally red brick workers' cottages adjacent to its east side formed a little square.

Dobson's capacity, even willingness, to work in an eclectic way seems to have proved an asset when he came to execute commissions, in sharply differing styles, for rival factions of the medical fraternity of Newcastle upon Tyne. In 1851 the School of Medicine and Surgery, founded seventeen years before, moved into a new classical Barber-Surgeons' Hall by Dobson in Victoria Street; paid for by the railway company, whose expansion to the Manors had necessitated the demolition of the original Hall, it was a major essay in his Italianate mode and one of his most dignified and successful later works, though marred by the ugly brick extensions now surrounding it.

The Italian Renaissance style had been popularised by Sir Charles Barry during the 1830s as the Greek Revival waned; more flexible and potentially ornate, it was developed by architects like Professor C.R. Cockerell whose own architecture combined Greek, Roman and Renaissance elements (as did Dobson's Central Station schemes). Cockerell and his followers at the Royal Academy, such as Dobson's son in law Sydney Smirke, did much to ensure that classicism remained an important alternative to the Gothic Revival, Renaissance forms becoming especially favoured during the 1850s and '60s for the large numbers of new public buildings such as banks, clubs, offices, libraries, museums and town halls. A Newcastle example was one of Dobson's last completed works, the Gas Company Office in Neville Street of 1861-62, which was adapted to a corner site having a rusticated ground floor with arched windows and rectangular windows above, surmounted by a cornice with large brackets, below a balustrade.

The Barber-Surgeons' Hall is a detached rectangular building of two storeys, its principal or south facade being a symmetrical composition with five bays, the outer two projecting with rusticated quoins; this is completed by a large cornice, dwarf attic, and tall rusticated chimneys in the manner of Vanbrugh, now unfortunately taken down. The upper windows of the central section form an arcade — contrasts of window type are typical of this style — with keystones decorated with the Aesculapian snakes, while in the spandrels are the historic armorial emblems of the Barber-Surgeons' Company, in the form of heraldic shields. The first floor contained lecture and dissecting rooms, and a large museum, illuminated also from above.

No sooner had the Hall been occupied than the profession split — two rival inaugural lectures were given on the 1st October, 1851 — with the majority party defecting to the historic Westmoreland House in Neville Street, to which they added their new College of Medicine in 1852[14]. No doubt a completely different image was necessary, and this time Dobson provided a long, low asymmetrical block with plate glass windows, but blending with Westmoreland House and 'suggesting collegiate architecture of the Tudor period'[15]; it was quaint enough, but much less impressive than the Barber-Surgeons' Hall, which in turn reflected the tradition of the original early 18th century Hall. The Colleges united in 1857 and the Barber-Surgeons' Hall, hitherto the 'College of Practical Science', became a school in 1862.

Renaissance classicism was beginning to be a significant element during the last decade of Dobson's work, and it is a pity he did not use the style more. Further examples include his design for the Warrington Museum and Library (1853) and St. Columba's Presbyterian church, North Shields (1856-57). The church, integrated into its setting in Northumberland Square by its plainer wings of brick, has a particularly dignified stone facade. This has five bays with Tuscan half-columns and, at the angles, pilasters supporting an entablature below cornice and balustrade, standing on a rusticated base.

The Warrington Museum and Library was one of the first rate-maintained municipal institutions of this kind, made possible by the Public Museums Act of 1845. Perhaps as a result of his more widespread renown after the opening of the Central Station, Newcastle, or because of a family connection between patrons, Dobson was commissioned by the Council to prepare plans in 1853; the result was a vigorous if idiosyncratic design which if executed would have been one of his most monumental public works. A site was donated by John Wilson-Patten, M.P., but sufficient funds could not be raised and the architect was paid off with a sum actually less than he had charged[16]; a local builder was then employed to produce a more economical design. Dobson had proposed a three storey classical building with basement, in brick with stone dressings, having a double height lecture theatre (he also designed a lecture theatre for the Newcastle Literary and Philosophical Society in 1859), library

NEWCASTLE-UPON-TYNE COLLE
IN CONNECTION WITH THE UNIVERSIT

103

102

102. St. Columbia's Presbyterian Church, North Shields, 1856—7

103. College of Medicine, Newcastle upon Tyne, 1852. From an engraving (Laing Art Gallery, Newcastle upon Tyne)

104. Warrington Museum and Library, Cheshire, 1853. From a watercolour by Dobson (Warrington Library)

104

NE.

accommodation at ground floor level above an architectural antiquities room, and the main museum galleries on the top two floors[17]. It would have had heavily rusticated pilasters, arches and quoins, and at the upper level panels with relief sculpture instead of windows, the upper galleries being once again top lit. Strangely, it would have had a cornice more medieval than classical in form — a solecism, but perhaps intended to symbolise the range of antiquities displayed. The building as built in 1855-57 is an almost unrecognisably simplified version of this design. Again one of Dobson's most ambitious and carefully considered schemes had not been carried out.

Notes

1 *AA*, new series, vol. XI, p.177.

2 *Op. cit.*, new series, vol. IV, p.153.

3 See G.H. Hume, *The History of the Newcastle Infirmary*, 1906.

4 See *Report of the Deputation of the Building Committee of the Newcastle upon Tyne Infirmary*, 1852, (in the Literary and Philosophical Society of Newcastle upon Tyne, 'Tracts', 8vo series, vol. 135 no. 10, and vol. 237 no. 5).

5 See Minutes of the Newcastle Council, 4 August 1858.

6 *Ibid.*, 6 May 1857.

7 *Ibid.*, 1 July 1857, and 7 July 1858, reproducing first and second reports by Dobson.

8 J. Dobson *Description and Plan of New Streets and Buildings on the Sites of the Late Fires etc.*, 1854.

9 Minutes of the Newcastle Council, 7 May 1856.

10 Dobson, pp.34 and 70; this is probably the visit supposedly made in connection with his work at Friedelhausen discussed in Chapter 6.

11 For a discussion of Sir Hedworth Williamson's projects see P. Emmerson, 'The Williamson Family of Whitburn, some aspects of its History', unpublished dissertation for Honours Degree in History and English, Sunderland Polytechnic, 1986.

12 See Fordyce, II, p.480.

13 Dobson's plan of 1857 is with the Whitby Literary and Philosophical Society.

14 See G.G. Turner, *Newcastle upon Tyne School of Medicine, 1834—1934*, 1934, pp.35 *et seq.*

15 *The Builder*, vol. X, 1852, p.658.

16 See Warrington Council Minutes, 1853—1854, especially 9 May 1853 and 5 December 1854.

17 Dobson's plans are in the Library and Museum, Warrington.

IX *Postscript*

Dobson's severe stroke of 1862, at the age of 74, brought his long career to a sudden end. He retired briefly to Ryton but returned to his New Bridge Street house in Newcastle shortly before his death on 8th January 1865. In his will he left his 'household furniture and stores plate linen and pictures' to his daughter Margaret, all his 'plans drawing office furniture and drawing and other instruments' to his son John and all his 'books prints and sketches' to his son in law Sydney Smirke. Margaret Dobson gave her framed architectural perspectives to the Laing Art Gallery in Newcastle upon Tyne in 1905; the locations of John Dobson jnr.'s plans and most of Sydney Smirke's sketches remain sadly unknown to the authors. For a short while his practice was carried on by Thomas Austin who later formed a successful Newcastle partnership with R.J. Johnson.

Without doubt the most eminent architect to be born and to have worked in the North East of England, John Dobson had had a lengthy career spanning parts of both the Georgian and Victorian epochs. As we have seen, this reflected not only changes in architectural fashion but also the major social and economic developments of the time, and he worked substantially for the new entrepreneurial middle classes, establishing themselves through commerce and industry on Tyneside and elsewhere. A sense of tradition, a feeling for the relationship of a building to its site, and engineering skill underlined his facility in working within the numerous styles then considered appropriate, and in designing the vast range of building types which he undertook. Indeed, it is the quantity and variety of his architecture which strikes an observer reviewing his career, rather than any particular stylistic theme.

Like many early 19th century architects, and for that matter more than most, he avoided specialising in a single style, believing that a range of styles could be used, according to the building specimen or type. He held 'that to every building of importance, there ought to belong a special character, based upon the purpose for which the building was designed, and that it was the part of the architect fully to develop this character in his work'[1]. Dobson did not get involved in controversies such as the 'Battle of the Styles' between the Victorian Goths and Classicists, or become immersed in the complex architectural theories of the day. He was a pragmatic man, his dispassionate temperament being many times remarked upon.

Themes in his work are less to do with style than with more general qualities such as the felicitous siting of his buildings and their excellent construction, particularly in stone; the masonry of his finest works could hardly be surpassed. Dobson employed a variety of building firms, but he favoured on several occasions a few particularly expert men, such as the plasterer Ralph Dodds, the carpenter Thomas Hall, the mason and contractor Robert Robson, and his own son in law Gibson Kyle. Robert Wallace, initially a builder, was employed by Dobson as his Lilburn clerk of works, and, as we have seen, became the Town Surveyor of Newcastle upon Tyne. To have worked for Dobson became a qualification in itself, and masons who had done so sometimes advertised in this way. William Wailes, the notable stained glass designer was also closely associated with Dobson's work.

Even Dobson's most modest works usually make something of their site. When engaged to make a design, it was his custom, we are told, to 'make himself thoroughly acquainted with the *genius loci* from every point of view'[2]. His love of nature, and early training as a gardener, may give some truth to the claim that he almost preferred the landscape and 'dressed gardens' surrounding his works to the buildings themselves[3]. Certainly his Gothic and Tudor country houses show a complete assimilation of the Picturesque.

Another important theme in his work is its emphasis upon the technical and functional aspects of design. We have examined his meticulous researches into hospital and prison types, for example, and the main topics of his inaugural Presidential Address to the Northern Architectural Association in 1859, apart from the growth of the profession itself, are his improvement in the comfort of country houses, his practical adaptation of castellated forms for prison architecture, and his ingenious and economical design for the Central Station roof. One can imagine the zeal with

105. John Dobson in middle age. From an oil painting (Laing Art Gallery, Newcastle upon Tyne)

which he must have worked on this, with Hawks and Crawshay, and it is significant that at the Great Exhibition he exhibited not only models of the Station itself, but also a rolling machine, designed by one of their engineers, used in rolling iron for the principals of its roof[4]. Also at the Station, he successfully planned for the increase in traffic that was bound to come.

Although a sensible, and genial man, and robust and vigorous in physique — he enjoyed boxing and fencing in his youth — Dobson had 'the fastidiousness of a retiring nature'[5]. He was not a businessman and seems to have lacked the ultimate degree of ambition necessary to fully promote himself. Thus he failed to push through his early plans for the rebuilding of central Newcastle, leaving the entrepreneur Richard Grainger to implement a modified version of the scheme. However, as we have seen, he enjoyed a favoured position with the Newcastle Council in later years. Dobson had a talent for town planning, and Newcastle in particular would have been an even finer city if more of his improvements had been carried out (and fewer of his executed buildings destroyed!).

Dobson may have been too unambitious to set up in London at the start, though apparently encouraged to do so by well connected friends[6]. Nor did he enter any of the great national architectural competitions, though he did enter several local ones. Rarely did he exhibit at the Royal Academy, though again he did so locally. However, the capital had been amply provided with architects in about 1810, and it was probably an astute move to establish practice in the North East. Here at first, he later recalled[7], he enjoyed with his friend Ignatius Bonomi 'the somewhat barren dignity' of being one of only two professional architects between Edinburgh and York. This is significant: he had been determined to establish himself as an architect alone, as opposed to the builder-architects practising in Newcastle at that time. His ungenerous remark about David Stephenson (that he was not an accomplished architect)[8] must be explained by the fact that Dobson wanted to emphasise his own role in the development of the architectural profession.

Early in his career commissions were few, but soon a situation underpinned by the expanding commerce and industry of the region led to his being prolifically employed. His patrons can be divided into four interconnected groups. There were the aristocrats such as Sir Jacob Astley, Lord Londonderry, and the Earl of Strathmore, all of whom had industrial interests too. The favour of the Duke of Northumberland helped provide the indirect patronage of County public works. Then there were the landed gentry, including the Blacketts, the Collingwoods, the Ordes, and the Riddells, and William Lawson of Longhirst who made money from coal as well. An established Newcastle oligarchy for whom Dobson worked consisted of men like the reformer Sir Thomas Burdon (Mayor in 1810), the solicitor Armorer Donkin, Sir John Fife and T.E. Headlam of the medical establishment and the M.P. John Hodgson Hinde — all private patrons and useful in the choice of his designs for civic works. His largest group of clients were the middle class bankers, merchants and industrialists (who married into the other categories whenever possible). Sir William (later Lord) Armstrong and George Hudson are the best known of these, but also important were the Carlisle cotton manufacturer Peter Dixon, the banker Thomas Fenwick, and the Cookson family of glass and chemical manufacturers on Tyneside. Minor figures of this kind included R. Plummer (flax), Michael Robson (docks), and the tobacco merchant Benjamin Sorsbie. Most of Dobson's work outside the North East was gained through family connections with the above, but he did achieve a more national reputation after the opening of the Newcastle Central Station, for which he presented drawings to the Queen, as well as exhibiting designs in 1851.

Obviously Dobson must have been an exceptionally dedicated man. He tells how in his youth he gained inspiration from the aged Benjamin West, still working a few days before he died[9], and Dobson himself retired only after his stroke in 1862. Only a few weeks after the death of his son in the Quayside explosion of 1854, a blow from which he never really recovered, he was planning the redevelopment of the very locality where the unfortunate young man had been killed. 'I still can feel the same anxiety to improve, and the same pleasure and delight in my profession that I felt when I was but a boy' he told his younger colleagues, many of whom he helped and encouraged, in 1859[10]. It was a legacy of professional integrity, rather than any particular stylistic influence that Dobson left, though the long survival of classicism in the North East can be partly attributed to him.

Dobson headed a substantial office with clerks, draughtsmen and pupils who assisted with design, such as the successful Newcastle architect Thomas Oliver (from 1815-21). Later pupils included Gibson Kyle, James Moffat, Thomas Prosser, and George Ridley (later chief clerk to Sydney Smirke). Others were E.R. Robson, a nationally known School Board architect, and Thomas Austin, who completed some of Dobson's works before joining up with R.J. Johnson, who had returned to the North East after working under Gilbert Scott. Johnson and Robson became leading exponents of the 'Queen Anne' style. Two of Dobson's sons were also assistants: John jnr., employed from 1854 after his brother Alexander's death, while Alexander, a pupil of Sydney Smirke, had clearly been destined to take over his father's practice. Possible hopes of an architectural dynasty were not to be. Dobson had married in 1816 Isabella Rutherford of Gateshead, herself a talented amateur artist; it was their eldest daughter, also called Isabella, who married Sydney Smirke in 1840.

Architects contemporary with Dobson on Tyneside included Oliver, the Greens, John and William Stokoe jnr., and later John Johnstone and William Parnell. More in touch with the national scene than the others, however, Dobson has been equated with Barry, Blore, Burn and Salvin in terms of country house architecture during the 1830s[11] — though Dobson was more regionally based. In 1845 he became a Fellow of the Institute of British Architects, proposed by Donaldson, Salvin and Smirke; how he must have approved of the declaration he was obliged to sign: 'I will not have any interest or participation in any trade contract or materials, supplied at any works, the execution of which I may be engaged to superintend'.

Dobson's draughtsmanship has long been much admired. He had a meticulous, fine-lined style, and in his presentation watercolours the buildings drawn by him were combined with landscape and figures by his collaborators, such as T.M. Richardson or, more usually, J.W. Carmichael. From an early age he determined to produce the most attractive, even glamorous presentation of his designs. However, although he was an early exponent of the form, the tradition that he was the first to exhibit coloured architectural perspectives at the Royal Academy or elsewhere, is incorrect.

The general characteristics of Dobson's architecture were 'adaptability, patience, constructive imagination, and intelligence of the *genius loci*'[12]. He achieved a remarkable level of competence throughout his long career; he was not so much an innovator as a consolidator of current styles. His architecture has a certain distinctive heaviness and strength which is invariably recognisable, at least in the case of work done before the bewildering eclecticism of his final phase. His ability lay less in forming delicate details (with some noteworthy exceptions) than in the composition of mass, particularly when expressed in block like forms. Hence the Greek Revival and neoclassical styles provided opportunities for his talent at its best. His Gothic, though important to him, lacked the passion of his better classical work; he never became a doctrinaire revivalist like Butterfield or Street. There are peaks of achievement in his career. Longhirst is as fine or finer than anything of that time, while the Central Station as proposed was a magnificent design — in the spirit of Vanbrugh according to a critic of the day[13]. Its failure to be built typifies the many disappointments and frustrations of Dobson's professional life, stoically endured.

Singularly expressive of Dobson are his Jesmond Cemetery Chapels and Gates. For J.C. Loudon the composition was the most appropriate he had seen[14], while to a modern critic it is 'grandly original, severely noble and uncompromisingly stark'[15]. Sir Albert Richardson found 'superlative merit in its design'[16]. No more appropriate resting place for the architect could have been imagined than the cemetery he had designed himself. He was an immensely respected and important provincial architect of considerable national renown.

Notes

1 Dobson, p.19.

2 *Ibid.*, p.14.

3 See obituary of Dobson in the *NDJ*, 9 January, 1865.

4 See *Official Descriptive and Illustrated Catalogue* of the Great Exhibition of 1851, p.323; the machine was designed by Thomas Charlton.

5 Dobson, p.65.

6 *Ibid.*, p.15.

7 Wilkes, p.104.

8 *Ibid.*, p.103.

9 *Ibid.*, p.102.

10 *Ibid.*

11 See D. Watkin, *The English Vision*, 1982, p.133—134.

12 A.E. Richardson, *Monumental Classic Architecture in Great Britain and Ireland in the Nineteenth Century*, 1914, p.87.

13 See obituary of Dobson in *The Building News*, 13 January, 1865, quoting a review in the *Athenaeum* of Dobson's designs exhibited at the Royal Academy.

14 Quoted in J. S. Curl, 'Northern Cemetery under Threat', in *CL.*, 2 July, 1981, p.68.

15 *Ibid.*

16 A.E. Richardson, *op. cit.*, p.87.

CATALOGUE OF WORKS

This chronological list of Dobson's work includes unexecuted designs and has been compiled from contemporary newspapers and other sources, the obituary in the Newcastle Daily Journal and Margaret Dobson's *Memoir*. Wherever possible works listed in the *Memoir* have been confirmed by contemporary sources, but some have not. The references quoted are the earliest evidence of Dobson's authorship. Those works which bear only a reference to the *Memoir* [e.g. Dobson, p119] require further substantiation.

The authors would be very pleased to hear of any corrections or additions to the catalogue, preferably supported by contemporary evidence.

ROYAL JUBILEE SCHOOL, CITY ROAD, NEWCASTLE UPON TYNE, classical, 1810 [Mackenzie, 1827, p452; drawing in Laing Art Gallery]

SCOTTISH PRESBYTERIAN CHURCH, HOWARD STREET, NORTH SHIELDS, TYNE AND WEAR (N), classical, 1811 [*NC*, 3 Aug 1811]

WESLEYAN METHODIST CHAPEL, NEW ROAD, NEWCASTLE UPON TYNE, classical, 1812, dem. [*NC*, 25 Jly 1812]

FIELD HOUSE, GATESHEAD, TYNE AND WEAR (D), classical house for George Barras, 1813, dem. 1931 [Manders, *History of Gateshead*, 1973, p133; Dobson, p73]

BRADLEY HALL, RYTON, TYNE AND WEAR, alterations to mid 18th century house for 1st Lord Ravensworth, c.1813 [*NDJ*, 16 Jan 1865]

CHEESEBURN GRANGE, NORTHUMBERLAND, substantial Gothic remodelling of 18th century house for Ralph Riddell, c.1813 [*NDJ*, 16 Jan 1865; drawings coll. Major Philip Riddell]

GIBSIDE, TYNE AND WEAR (D), proposed minor alterations and addition of conservatory to Jacobean house for 10th Earl of Strathmore, 1814 [drawings in DCRO (D/St/X46a,81)]

HOUSE OF CORRECTION, TYNEMOUTH, TYNE AND WEAR (N), additions, 1814 [Dobson, p118]

HOWDON DOCKS, WALLSEND, TYNE AND WEAR (N), 1814 [Dobson, p127]

THEATRE ROYAL, MOSLEY STREET, NEWCASTLE UPON TYNE, embellishments and illuminations, 1814 [*NA*, 17 May 1814]

WALLSEND, TYNE AND WEAR (N), staithes, 1814 [Dobson, p125]

SEATON DELAVAL, NORTHUMBERLAND, proposed alterations and additions to Vanbrugh's 18th century house for Sir Jacob Henry Astley, 1814—7 [drawings at Seaton Delaval]

BACKWORTH HALL, NORTHUMBERLAND, alterations to William Newton's late 18th century house for R. Grey, 1815 [*NDJ*, 16 Jan 1865]

BLACKETT STREET, NEWCASTLE UPON TYNE, survey and valuation for Blackett Family, 1815 [drawing NCRO (ZBL 62/4)]

FALLODEN HALL, EMBLETON, NORTHUMBERLAND, additions for Sir George Grey, Bt., 1815, rebuilt early 20th century [*NDJ*, 16 Jan 1865]

HAMSTERLEY HALL, COUNTY DURHAM, alterations for R.S. Surtees, 1815 [*NDJ*, 16 Jan 1865]

MANOR OFFICE, HEXHAM, NORTHUMBERLAND, conversion for Col. Beaumont, 1815 [*NDJ*, 16 Jan 1865]

PRESTWICK LODGE, PONTELAND, NORTHUMBERLAND, classical house for Percival Fenwick, 1815 [*NC*, 9 Jun 1815]

UNTHANK HALL, NORTHUMBERLAND, additions for Robert Pearson, 1815 [*NDJ*, 16 Jan 1865]

WATERVILLE HOUSE, NORTH SHIELDS, TYNE AND WEAR (N), house for R. Rippon, 1815, dem. [*NDJ*, 16 Jan 1865]

CRAMLINGTON HALL, NORTHUMBERLAND, classical house for A.M. de C. Lawson, c.1815, dem. 1950s [*NDJ*, 16 Jan 1865]

ALL SAINTS' CHURCH, NEWCASTLE UPON TYNE, repairs to David Stephenson's 1787—97, church, 1816 [Mackenzie 1827, p305]

BENWELL GROVE, NEWCASTLE UPON TYNE, house for Charles Cook, 1816, dem. [*NDJ*, 16 Jan 1865]

ELAND HALL, PONTELAND, NORTHUMBERLAND, house for William Barkley, 1816 [Dobson, p76]

MINSTERACRES HALL, NORTHUMBERLAND, additions to late 18th century house for George Silvertop, 1816 [*NDJ*, 16 Jan 1865]

NORTH SHIELDS, TYNE AND WEAR (N), dock for Michael Robson, 1816 [*NDJ*, 16 Jan 1865]

NORTH SHIELDS, TYNE AND WEAR (N), docks for Mr Blackburn, 1816 [Dobson, p127]

PERCY TENANTRY COLUMN, ALNWICK, NORTHUMBERLAND, unexecuted design, 1816 [press cutting 4 June 1816 in Alnwick Castle Collection (DWS, Northum. 187A/151)]

TYNE BREWERY, NEWCASTLE UPON TYNE, 1816 [Dobson, p127]

WHICKHAM, TYNE AND WEAR (D), house for J. Errington, 1816 [Dobson, p76]

STRAWBERRY PLACE, NEWCASTLE UPON TYNE, house for J. Harvey, c.1816 [*NDJ*, 16 Jan 1865]

BOLAM, NORTHUMBERLAND, laying out of gardens and lake for Hon. W.H. Beresford 1816—18 [affidavit in NCRO (ZMI B13/X11)]

AXWELL PARK, TYNE AND WEAR (D), alterations to James Paine's house, including a garden temple, for Sir John Clavering, 1817 [*NDJ*, 16 Jan 1865]

BELFORD HALL, NORTHUMBERLAND, alterations and additions, including north entrance and wings to James Paine's house, for William Clark, 1817 [*NDJ*, 16 Jan 1865]

CUSTOMS HOUSE, GLASGOW, alterations, 1817, dem. [*NDJ*, 16 Jan 1865]

CUSTOMS HOUSE, LIVERPOOL, alterations, 1817, dem. c.1830 [*NDJ*, 16 Jan 1865]

CUSTOMS HOUSE, NEWCASTLE UPON TYNE, alterations, 1817, dem. c.1840 [*NDJ*, 16 Jan 1865]

JESMOND GROVE, NEWCASTLE UPON TYNE, house for James Losh, 1817 [Dobson, p77]

PERCY STREET, NEWCASTLE UPON TYNE, proposed crescent off Percy Street, 1817 [*NDJ*, 29 Mar 1817]

PRIORY CHURCH OF ST. ANDREW, HEXHAM, NORTHUMBERLAND, proposed restoration of east wall, 1817 [*NDJ*, 16 Jan 1865]

PRIORY, TYNEMOUTH, TYNE AND WEAR (N), proposed restoration, 1817, not carried out [*NDJ*, 16 Jan 1865]

ST. NICHOLAS'S, NEWCASTLE UPON TYNE, installation of heating by stoves, 1817 [*NDJ*, 16 Jan 1865]

SCHOOL, PONTELAND, NORTHUMBERLAND, 1817 [Dobson, p115]

SOUTH SHIELDS, TYNE AND WEAR (D), glassworks for Isaac Cookson, 1817 [Dobson, p127]

THEATRE ROYAL, NEWCASTLE UPON TYNE, remodelling of David Stephenson's 1787 entrance hall, 1817, dem. c.1835 [*Durham County Advertiser*, 9 Jan 1818]

TYNEMOUTH CASTLE, TYNE AND WEAR (N), fortifications, 1817 [Dobson, p128]

VILLA REALE, NEWCASTLE UPON TYNE, classical villa for Capt. John Dutton, 1817 [*NDJ*, 16 Jan 1865]

WEST JESMOND HOUSE, NEWCASTLE UPON TYNE, Gothic villa for Sir Thomas Burdon, 1817 [*NDJ*, 16 Jan 1865]

DOXFORD HALL, NORTHUMBERLAND, classical house for William Taylor, 1817—8 [*NDJ*, 16 Jan 1865]

BLACK DENE HOUSE, NEWCASTLE UPON TYNE, Gothic house for Dr. Thomas Emerson Headlam, 1818, rebuilt by Dobson for Thomas Cruddas, 1851, and by Richard Norman Shaw, 1870—1885, and F.W. Rich, 1896—7 [*NDJ*, 16 Jan 1865]

CHEESEBURN GRANGE, NORTHUMBERLAND, restoration of chapel for Ralph Riddell 1818, replaced by Hansom c.1860 [*NDJ*, 16 Jan 1865]

106 GOSFORTH PARK, NEWCASTLE UPON TYNE, additions, including entrance gates, to James Paine's house for Ralph Brandling, 1818 [*NDJ*, 16 Jan 1865]

106

JESMOND VILLA (or HOUSE) NEWCASTLE UPON TYNE, additions to classical house for Armorer Donkin, 1818 [Dobson, p77]

107 ST. NICHOLAS'S, GOSFORTH, NEWCASTLE UPON TYNE, additions, Tuscan, 1818, subsequently further enlarged [*NC*, 18 Jly 1818; drawing in NCRO (1875/A/50)]

107

SANDYFORD BRIDGE, NEWCASTLE UPON TYNE, 1818 [Dobson, p128]

SEXTON'S COTTAGE, ST. NICHOLAS'S, GOSFORTH, NEWCASTLE UPON TYNE, Tudor, 1818, dem. [drawing at St. Nicholas's Church]

WALLINGTON HALL, NORTHUMBERLAND, 'Large additions to Museum' for John Trevelyan, 1818 [*NDJ*, 16 Jan 1865]

GIBSIDE, TYNE AND WEAR (D), unknown work c.1818 for which Dobson paid £50 [account in DCRO (D/St/V1513 pp14,15)]

TOBACCO WAREHOUSE, NEWCASTLE UPON TYNE, for Benjamin Sorsbie, 1818—19 [*NC*, 13 Jun 1818; *NCh*, 2 Jan 1819]

CHIPCHASE CASTLE, NORTHUMBERLAND, alterations, including some refenestration, to 17th century house for John Reed, 1819 [*NDJ*, 16 Jan 1865]

CLERGY JUBILEE SCHOOL, CARLIOL SQUARE, NEWCASTLE UPON TYNE, classical, 1819, dem. [*NC*, 22 May 1819]

HAMSTERLEY, COUNTY DURHAM, corn mill for R.S. Surtees, 1819 [*NC*, 1 May 1819]

HEBBURN HALL, TYNE AND WEAR (D), alterations to 17th and 18th century house for Cuthbert Ellison, 1819 [Dobson, p80]

HEXHAM ABBEY HOUSE, NORTHUMBERLAND, alterations for T.R. Beaumont, 1819 [Dobson, p79]

PRESTON VILLA, NORTH SHIELDS, TYNE AND WEAR (N), house for John Fenwick 1819, dem. [Dobson, p79]

ROCK TOWER, NORTHUMBERLAND, Gothic additions to and restoration of 16th and 17th century house for Charles Bosanquet, 1819 [Dobson, p91]

ST. JOHN'S, ST. JOHN LEE, NORTHUMBERLAND, restoration, 1819, substantially altered 1885 [*NCh*, 13 Feb 1819]

ST. MARY'S, WHICKHAM, TYNE AND WEAR (D), restoration, 1819, subsequently rebuilt [Dobson, p101]

ST. ANDREW'S, WHITBURN, TYNE AND WEAR (D), restoration, 1819 [Dobson, p100]

WEST CHIRTON HOUSE, NORTH SHIELDS, TYNE AND WEAR (N), house for Michael Robson, 1819, dem. [Dobson, p80]

ST. NICHOLAS'S CHARITY SCHOOL, NEWCASTLE UPON TYNE, 1819—20 [Mackenzie 1827, p446]

AYDON CASTLE, NORTHUMBERLAND, restorations for Sir Edward Blackett, 1820 [Dobson, p81]

BIDDLESTONE HALL, NORTHUMBERLAND, additions to 18th century house for W. Selby, 1820, dem. 1960s [*NDJ*, 16 Jan 1865]

BROOME PARK, NORTHUMBERLAND, alterations and additions to late 18th century house for William Burrell, 1820, dem. 1853 [*NDJ*, 16 Jan 1865]

CASTLE, NEWCASTLE UPON TYNE, proposed conversion to prison and magistrates courts, c.1820 [Mackenzie 1827, p202]

PONTELAND RECTORY, NORTHUMBERLAND, alterations, c.1820? [*NDJ*, 16 Jan 1865]

ARCOT HALL, DUDLEY, NORTHUMBERLAND, additions to 18th century house for George Shum Storey, 1820s [*NDJ*, 16 Jan 1865]

CHESTERHILL, BELFORD, NORTHUMBERLAND, plain classical farmhouse, 1820s [*NDJ*, 16 Jan 1865]

HAWTHORN DENE HOUSE, COUNTY DURHAM, Gothic house for Major Anderson, 1821, remodelled by Thomas Moore, c.1850, ruinous [*NDJ*, 16 Jan 1865]

SOUTH HILL HOUSE, PLAWSWORTH, COUNTY DURHAM, classical house rebuilt for Thomas Fenwick, 1821, altered [Dobson, p82]

GAOL, CARLISLE, CUMBRIA, unbuilt design, probably castellated, 1822 [*Carlisle Patriot*, 3 Mar and 17 Aug 1822]

GAOL AND SESSIONS HOUSE, MORPETH, NORTHUMBERLAND, castellated, for County of Northumberland, 1822—8, partly dem. [*NC*, 10 Aug 1822; drawing in Laing Art Gallery]

GAOL, CARLIOL SQUARE, NEWCASTLE UPON TYNE, castellated, 1822—8, dem. c.1929 [*NC*, 26 Oct 1822; plans and specifications in TWA (No. 279/1)]

HOUSE OF CORRECTION, HEXHAM, NORTHUMBERLAND, alterations and additions, 1822, dem. [*NC*, 17 Aug 1822]

ACTON HOUSE, NORTHUMBERLAND, minor alterations for Major de Lisle, 1823 dem. [*NDJ*, 16 Jan 1865]

FLOTTERTON HOUSE, NORTHUMBERLAND, for C. Weallands, 1823 [Mackenzie 1827, p485]

GATESHEAD, TYNE AND WEAR (D), house for R. Plummer, 1823 [*NDJ*, 16 Jan 1865]

NEWTON-ON-THE-MOOR, NORTHUMBERLAND, house for Thomas Jamieson, 1823 [*NDJ*, 16 Jan 1865]

PRISON, BELFORD, NORTHUMBERLAND, Tudor, for County of Northumberland, 1823 [*NCh*, 22 Nov 1823]

PRISON, WOOLER, NORTHUMBERLAND, for County of Northumberland, 1823 [*NCh*, 22 Nov 1823]

SWANSFIELD HOUSE, ALNWICK, NORTHUMBERLAND, alterations (?) to plain classical house for Henry Collingwood Selby, 1823, dem. 1975 [Dobson, p83]

NEWBROUGH HOUSE, NORTHUMBERLAND, classical house for Richard Lambert (?), c.1823 [*NDJ*, 16 Jan 1865]

NEW BRIDGE STREET, NEWCASTLE UPON TYNE, Dobson's own house, 1823, and other classical 'detached villas' on the north side of the street, including Ridley Villas? 1823—4 [*NCh*, 29 Mar 1823; *NC*, 7 Feb 1824; Mackenzie 1827, p189]

108 ST. NICHOLAS'S, NEWCASTLE UPON TYNE, restoration of north transept window, 1823—4 [Mackenzie 1827, p248]

108

FISHMARKET etc., NEWCASTLE UPON TYNE, classical addition to Guildhall, 1823—6 [Mackenzie 1827, p217]

WEST JESMOND HOUSE, NEWCASTLE UPON TYNE, Gothic additions to Dobson's house of 1817, for Richard Burdon Sanderson, 1823—7 [Dobson, p83]

MITFORD HALL, NORTHUMBERLAND, classical house for Bertram Osbaldeston Mitford, 1823—8 [*NDJ*, 16 Jan 1865; Hodgson, II.2., p67]

SEAHAM, COUNTY DURHAM, town planned for 3rd Marquess of Londonderry, 1823—8 [*NC*, 6 Dec 1828; drawings DRCO (D/Lo/P596/1—8)]

BLACKETT STREET, NEWCASTLE UPON TYNE, 1824 [Mackenzie 1827, pp188—9]

HOUSE OF CORRECTION, ALNWICK, NORTHUMBERLAND, additions, for County of Northumberland, 1824 [*NCh*, 8 May 1824]

LONGHIRST HALL, NORTHUMBERLAND, classical house for William Lawson, 1824 [Hodgson, II.2, p159]

LUNATIC ASYLUM, BATH LANE, NEWCASTLE UPON TYNE, additions, 1824 [Mackenzie 1827, pp.525—6]

NEWTON-ON-THE-MOOR, NORTHUMBERLAND, 'Farm Offices' for Thomas Cook, 1824 [*NC*, 20 Mar 1824]

RIVER TYNE, NEWCASTLE UPON TYNE, 'plans and sections' for the Corporation, 1824 [*NDJ*, 16 Jan 1865]

ROTHBURY, NORTHUMBERLAND, 'mansion house with offices', 1824 [*NC*, 3 Apr 1824]

NEWCASTLE UPON TYNE, proposal for redevelopment of central Newcastle, c.1824—5 [Mackenzie 1827, p200]

HAMSTERLEY, COUNTY DURHAM, Gothic bridge, 1825 [Dobson, p129]

HARBOTTLE, NORTHUMBERLAND, bridge, 1825 [Dobson, p129]

INDEPENDENT CHAPEL, SUNDERLAND, TYNE AND WEAR (D), 1825 [*NDJ*, 16 Jan 1865]

LYING-IN HOSPITAL, NEWCASTLE UPON TYNE, Gothic, 1825 [Mackenzie 1827, p518]

NUNNYKIRK HALL, NORTHUMBERLAND, substantial classical remodelling of 18th century house for William Orde, 1825 [*NDJ*, 16 Jan 1865; Hodgson, II.1, p330]

ST. MICHAEL'S, ALNWICK, NORTHUMBERLAND, restoration, 1825 [Dobson, p101]

SHAWDON HALL, NORTHUMBERLAND, alterations and additions, 1825 [*NDJ*, 16 Jan 1865]

CORN EXCHANGE, MIDDLE STREET, NEWCASTLE UPON TYNE, unexecuted Gothic (?) design, c.1825 [Mackenzie 1827, pp199—200]

ELLISON PLACE, NEWCASTLE UPON TYNE, house for David Cram, c.1825, dem. [Mackenzie 1827, p190]

NEWCASTLE UPON TYNE, proposed new road, squares, etc. from Blackett Street to West Road, c.1825 [Mackenzie 1827, p201]

TRAFALGAR STREET, NEWCASTLE UPON TYNE, c.1825 [see Chap. 8, note 4]

TRAFALGAR STREET, NEWCASTLE UPON TYNE, proposed extension to Quayside, c.1825 [Mackenzie 1827, p202]

ELDON SQUARE, NEWCASTLE UPON TYNE (including Northern Counties Club), classical facades to a plan by Thomas Oliver, for Richard Grainger, 1825—31, mostly dem. c.1970 [Oliver 1831, p97; Mackenzie 1827, p189]

PICTON PLACE, NEWCASTLE UPON TYNE, classical villas, inc. 'Prospect House', and one for William Todd, c.1825—30, all dem. [Dobson, p97]

BROOME PARK, NORTHUMBERLAND, 'Dwelling house near Broome Park', 1826 [*NC*, 22 Apr 1826]

GORTANLOISK, DUNOON, ARGYLLSHIRE, shooting lodge for Sir John Fife, 1826 [*NDJ*, 16 Jan 1865]

HALTWHISTLE VICARAGE, NORTHUMBERLAND, improvements for Rev. N.J. Hollongsworth, 1826 [*NDJ*, 16 Jan 1865]

HALTWHISTLE, NORTHUMBERLAND, bridge, 1826 [*NC*, 29 Apr 1826]

PRESBYTERIAN CHURCH, NORTH SHIELDS, TYNE AND WEAR (N), 1826 [Dobson, p102]

ST. JAMES'S PRESBYTERIAN CHAPEL, BLACKETT STREET, NEWCASTLE UPON TYNE, classical 1826, dem. 1859 [Mackenzie, 1827, p386]

SUMMERHILL PLACE, NEWCASTLE UPON TYNE, house, 1826 [*NC*, 11 Nov 1826]

COXLODGE, NEWCASTLE UPON TYNE, undetermined work for John Walker, c.1826 [*The Builder*, 14 Jan 1865; *NDJ*, 16 Jan 1865]

SCOTTISH PRESBYTERIAN CHURCH, MONKWEARMOUTH, TYNE AND WEAR (D), classical 1826—7, dem. [*NC*, 21 Jly 1827]

ST. CUTHBERT'S, GREENHEAD, NORTHUMBERLAND, Gothic, 1826—8, chancel added 1900 [*NDJ*, 16 Jan 1865; plans in ICBS (No. 766)]

ST. MARY'S, BELFORD, NORTHUMBERLAND, restoration and rebuilding, 1826—9 [*NDJ*, 16 Jan 1865; ground plan in ICBS (No. 756)]

BELLISTER CASTLE, NORTHUMBERLAND, alterations for John Kirsop, 1827, restored after a fire in 1901 [*NDJ*, 16 Jan 1865]

BOROUGHBRIDGE, NORTH YORKSHIRE, wooden bridge, 1827 [Dobson, p129]

CHAPEL, HEWORTH, TYNE AND WEAR (D), for 'Mr. Hall, viewer', 1827 [*NDJ*, 16 Jan 1865]

GRAMMAR SCHOOL, MORPETH, NORTHUMBERLAND, restoration, 1827 [*NC*, 24 Feb 1827]

QUAKERS' MEETING HOUSE, NEWCASTLE UPON TYNE, 1827 [Dobson, p102]

ST. NICHOLAS'S, NEWCASTLE UPON TYNE, restoration of steeple, 1827 [Sykes, ii, p213]

WALBOTTLE, NEWCASTLE UPON TYNE, bridge, 1827 [Dobson, p130]

NORTHERN ACADEMY OF ART, NEWCASTLE UPON TYNE, classical, 1827—8 [*Newcastle Magazine*, VI, 12, p570]

ST. THOMAS THE MARTYR, NEWCASTLE UPON TYNE, Gothic, 1827—30 [*NC*, 26 Jly 1827; perspective in Laing Art Gallery]

ARTHURS HILL, NEWCASTLE UPON TYNE, streets and elevations planned for Isaac Cookson, 1827—33 (John Street, Edward Street, William Street, etc) [TWA (1512)]

ANGERTON, NORTHUMBERLAND, repairs to 'Mansion House' including new chapel (?), 1828, dem. c.1840 [*NC*, 16 Aug 1828]

CHURCH AT GLOUCESTER, for J. Cargill, 1828 [*NDJ*, 16 Jan 1865]

CROSS, HOLY ISLAND, NORTHUMBERLAND, reconstruction, for H.C. Selby, 1828 [*NDJ*, 16 Jan 1865]

EARSDON, NORTHUMBERLAND, repairs to farm, 1828 [*NC*, 16 Aug 1828]

EDINBURGH, house for Charles Bruce, 1828 [Dobson, p85]

EMBLETON VICARAGE, NORTHUMBERLAND, substantial Tudor Gothic additions to pele tower for Rev. George Dixwell Grimes, 1828 [*NDJ*, 16 Jan 1865]

HALTWHISTLE, NORTHUMBERLAND, bridge, 1828 [*NCh*, 5 Apr 1828]

HARTBURN, NORTHUMBERLAND, repairs to farms, inc. Angerton (q.v.), 1828 [*NC*, 16 Aug 1828]

LONG BARTON, NORTHUMBERLAND, repairs to farms, 1828 [*NC*, 16 Aug 1828]

MAFTEN HALL, NORTHUMBERLAND, alterations (to the Dower House?) for Sir Edward Blackett, 1828 [Dobson, p84]

MORPETH, NORTHUMBERLAND, bridge at High Ford, 1828 [*NC*, 6 Apr 1828]

NEVILLE STREET, NEWCASTLE UPON TYNE, planned 1828, built c.1835 [*NDJ*, 16 Jan 1865]

PRESBYTERIAN CHAPEL, NORTH SHIELDS, TYNE AND WEAR (N), 1828, dem. [*NDJ*, 16 Jan 1865]

THE PRIORY CHURCH OF ST. ANDREW, HEXHAM, NORTHUMBERLAND, repair of east window, 1828 [Sykes ii, p225]

WOOLSINGTON HALL, TYNE AND WEAR (N), alterations for Matthew Bell, 1828 [Dobson, p85]

109 LILBURN TOWER, NORTHUMBERLAND, Tudor Gothic house for Henry Collingwood, 1828—9, altered by Dobson for E.J. Collingwood, 1843—4 [*NC*, 10 Jan 1829; perspective in Laing Art Gallery]

109

CASTLE HOUSE, HARBOTTLE, NORTHUMBERLAND, alterations for Thomas Fenwick Clennell, 1829 [Dobson, p86]

GLANTON PIKE, NORTHUMBERLAND, additions for Henry Collingwood, 1829 [*NDJ*, 16 Jan 1865]

RIDLEY HALL, NORTHUMBERLAND, alterations for John Davidson, 1829 [*NDJ*, 16 Jan 1865]

ST. JOHN'S, NEWCASTLE UPON TYNE, restoration, 1829 [Dobson, p104]

MORPETH, NORTHUMBERLAND, bridge, 1829—31 [Hodgson II.2, p426; *NCh*, 18 Jly 1829]

110 ST. MARY'S PLACE, NEWCASTLE UPON TYNE, Tudor terrace, from 1829 [*NCh*, 6 Jun 1829; *NC*, 20 Mar 1830]

110

ST. MARY'S, STAMFORDHAM, NORTHUMBERLAND, restoration, 1830 [Dobson, p104]

ST. MARY'S, WOODHORN, NORTHUMBERLAND, restoration, 1830 [Dobson, p104]

ST. NICHOLAS'S, WEST BOLDON, TYNE AND WEAR (D), addition of gallery, 1830 [*NC*, 31 Jly 1830]

SANDHILL, NEWCASTLE UPON TYNE, offices at north east end of Tyne Bridge, 1830 [*NC*, 19 Jun 1830]

TREWHITT HOUSE, NETHERTON, NORTHUMBERLAND, alterations? to classical house for John Smart, 1830 [Dobson, p86]

BURNHOPESIDE HALL, LANCHESTER, COUNTY DURHAM, classical house, c.1830 [stylistic attribution, Pevsner and Williamson, *Co. Durham*, 1983, p352]

GALLOWSHAW RIGG, NORTHUMBERLAND, house? for Sir Edward Blackett, Bt., c.1830? [*NDJ*, 16 Jan 1865]

TOLL HOUSE, BARRAS BRIDGE, NEWCASTLE UPON TYNE, Tudor, c.1830, dem. [*NDJ*, 16 Jan 1865]

UNIDENTIFIED DESIGN FOR A SMALL COUNTRY HOUSE, for Blackett Family, c.1830 [stylistic attribution; plans in NCRO (ZBL 269/72)]

BENWELL TOWER, NEWCASTLE UPON TYNE, rebuilt as castellated Tudor house for Thomas Crawhall, 1830—1; chapel added 1881 [*NDJ*, 16 Jan 1865; drawings in Private Collection]

BRINKBURN PRIORY HOUSE, NORTHUMBERLAND, large additions to house of c.1800 for Major Willam Hodgson-Cadogan, 1830—7 [*NDJ*, 16 Jan 1865; drawing in Laing Art Gallery]

BRINKBURN PRIORY, NORTHUMBERLAND, repairs to ruined priory for Major William Hodgson-Cadogan, c.1830—7, fully restored by Thomas Austin, 1858 [HMBCE guide, 1985]

NORTH ELSWICK HALL, NEWCASTLE UPON TYNE, house for B. Johnson, 1830s? [*NDJ*, 16 Jan 1865]

CASTLETON HOUSE, ROCKCLIFFE, CUMBRIA, alterations for George Gill Mounsey, 1831? [*NDJ*, 16 Jan 1865]

111 MARKET HOUSE, NEVILLE STREET, NEWCASTLE UPON TYNE, classical cattle market office and toll house, 1831 [*NDJ*, 16 Jan 1865]

111

NORTH SEATON HALL, NORTHUMBERLAND, estate buildings for J. N. Nicholson?, 1831 [*NC*, 21 May 1831]

SCHOOL, CHOLLERTON, NORTHUMBERLAND, Tudor, 1831, largely dem. [Dobson, p115]

SCHOOL, HENDON, SUNDERLAND, TYNE AND WEAR (D), 1831, dem. [Fordyce, II, p466]

ST. JAMES'S, BENWELL, TYNE AND WEAR (N), neo-Norman, 1831—2, much enlarged, [*NC*, 16 Apr 1831; drawings in RIBA (RAN/1/E/4/1—4)]

DARLINGTON, COUNTY DURHAM, house for J. Wilson, 1832 [*NDJ*, 16 Jan 1865]

MELDON PARK, NORTHUMBERLAND, classical house for Isaac Cookson, 1832 [*NDJ*, 16 Jan 1865; drawings in Laing Art Gallery]

ST. MATTHEW'S, DINNINGTON, NORTHUMBERLAND, Gothic, 1832 [*The Builder*, XXIII, 1865, p27]

SCHOOL, STAMFORDHAM, NORTHUMBERLAND, Tudor, 1832 [Dobson, p115]

112

112 ROYAL ARCADE, NEWCASTLE UPON TYNE, classical, for Richard Grainger, 1831—2, dem. 1963 [Dobson, p119; drawings Laing Art Gallery and Private Collection]

WHITBURN HALL, TYNE AND WEAR (D), alterations and additions to 17th and 18th century house for Sir Hedworth Williamson, Bt., 1832 and 1856?, dem. 1980 [*NDJ*, 16 Jan 1865]

113 ST. NICHOLAS'S, NEWCASTLE UPON TYNE, underpinning of tower, also addition with J. Green of north west and south west porches, 1832—4 [*AA*, 4th series, IX, p143]

113

CHESTERS, NORTHUMBERLAND, additions to John Carr's house for John Clayton, 1832—7, remodelled by R. Norman Shaw, 1893 [Dobson, p87]

CULLERCOATS, TYNE AND WEAR (N), building sites for sale to elevations by Dobson, 1833 [*NCh*, 16 Nov 1833]

BAPTIST CHAPEL, TUTHILL STAIRS, NEWCASTLE UPON TYNE, repairs and alterations to Elizabethan dwelling used as chapel, 1834, dem. [*NDJ*, 16 Jan 1865]

CHAPEL AT HOWDON DENE, TYNE AND WEAR (N), 1834 [*NDJ*, 16 Jan 1865]

114 GENERAL CEMETERY, GATESHEAD, TYNE AND WEAR (D), 1834 [*NC*, 11 Oct 1834]

HIGH WARDEN, HEXHAM, NORTHUMBERLAND, additions for John Errington, 1834 [Dobson, p89]

ST. CUTHBERT'S (RC), COWPEN, Nr. BLYTH, NORTHUMBERLAND, Gothic, 1834 [*NDJ*, 16 Jan 1865]

STAMFORDHAM VICARAGE, NORTHUMBERLAND, additions, c.1834 [Dobson, p115]

MARKETS, NEWCASTLE UPON TYNE, vegetable and butcher market and street facades (?) for Richard Granger, 1834—5 [drawings in Laing Art Gallery]

GENERAL CEMETERY, NEWCASTLE UPON TYNE, classical lodges, gates, etc. 1834—6 [*NC*, 29 Mar 1834]

GREY STREET, NEWCASTLE UPON TYNE, east side between High Bridge and Mosley Street, for Richard Grainger, 1834—7 [drawings in Laing Art Gallery, Getty Museum and Private Collection]

NEASHAM HALL, COUNTY DURHAM, large Elizabethan additions to 18th century house for Col. James Cookson, 1834—7, dem. 1970 [*NDJ*, 16 Jan 1865]

114

HOUSE OF CORRECTION, TYNEMOUTH, TYNE AND WEAR (N), additions, 1835 [*NC*, 31 Jan 1835]

MONKWEARMOUTH, TYNE AND WEAR (D), planning development of Monkwearmouth Shore and new road from bridge to North Quay, for Sir Hedworth Williamson, 1835 [*NJ*, 3 Oct 1835]

MORPETH, NORTHUMBERLAND, bridge at Low Ford, 1835 [*NC*, 2 May 1835]

ST. ANDREW'S, HARTBURN, NORTHUMBERLAND, addition of west gallery, 1835 [*NDJ*, 16 Jan 1865]

BLENKINSOPP HALL, NORTHUMBERLAND, large additions to early 19th century house for Col. J.B. Coulson, c.1835, removed mid 20th century [*NDJ*, 16 Jan 1865]

GREY MONUMENT, NEWCASTLE UPON TYNE, unsuccessful proposal, 1836 [*NC*, 20 Feb 1836]

POLICE OFFICES etc., MANOR CHARE, NEWCASTLE UPON TYNE, 1836 [*NC*, 23 Apr 1836]

115 ST. PAUL'S, WARWICK BRIDGE, CUMBRIA, neo-Norman, for Peter Dixon, 1836 [*NDJ*, 16 Jan 1865]

115

SUNDERLAND AND DURHAM JOINT STOCK BANK, MOSLEY STREET, NEWCASTLE UPON TYNE, 1836 [Dobson, p120]

TYNE TO DUNBAR RAILWAY, prospectus issued by Dobson, Matthias Dunn and Robert Hawthorn, 1836 [Tomlinson, *The Great Northern Railway*, 1914, p292]

116 ST. PAUL'S RECTORY, WARWICK BRIDGE, CUMBRIA, Tudor, c.1836 [attributed on grounds of proximity and style]

ELLISON SCHOOLS, GATESHEAD, TYNE AND WEAR (D), Tudor, 1836—7, dem. [*NCh*, 15 Oct 1836]

HOLY TRINITY, GATESHEAD, TYNE AND WEAR (D), formerly St. Edmund's Chapel, restoration 1836—7, greatly enlarged 1893 [*NCh*, 15 Oct 1836]

COACHMAKERS' MANUFACTORY, NEWCASTLE UPON TYNE, for Messrs. Atkinson and Philipson, 1837, dem. c.1920 [*NDJ*, 16 Jan 1865]

116

HOLME EDEN, WARWICK BRIDGE, CUMBRIA, Tudor-Gothic house for Peter Dixon, 1837, [*NDJ*, 16 Jan 1865; drawings in Private Collection and RIBA (G6/38/1—3)]

QUAYSIDE, NEWCASTLE UPON TYNE, new quay between Broad Chare and the Swirle 1837 [*NC*, 25 Aug 1837]

SAVINGS BANK, HEXHAM, NORTHUMBERLAND, classical, 1837 [*NC*, 7 July 1837]

WILLIAMSON MONUMENT, ST. NICHOLAS'S, NEWCASTLE UPON TYNE, classical, 1837 [*NC*, 23 Jun 1837]

MONKWEARMOUTH, TYNE AND WEAR (D), dock office, North Dock, for Sir Hedworth Williamson, c.1837, dem. [T. Corfe, *Buildings of Sunderland 1814— 1914*, p18]

PUBLIC BATHS, NORTHUMBERLAND ROAD, NEWCASTLE UPON TYNE, 1837—9 [*NJ*, 25 May 1839]

BEAUFRONT CASTLE, HEXHAM, NORTHUMBERLAND, Gothic house for William Cuthbert, incorporating an earlier house, 1837—41 [*NC*, 11 Mar 1837; drawings in Laing Art Gallery]

ST. MICHAEL'S, ALWINTON, NORTHUMBERLAND, restoration, 1838 [*NDJ*, 16 Jan 1865]

TYNEMOUTH, TYNE AND WEAR, 'CROWN HOTEL, BATHS, etc', 1838 [*NC*, 2 Nov 1830]

WYNYARD PARK, CLEVELAND (D), unidentified work following dismissal of Philip Wyatt by Lord Londonderry, 1838 [*CI*, 28 Aug 1986]

CRASTER TOWER, NORTHUMBERLAND, minor alterations to medieval and late 18th century house for Thomas Wood-Craster, 1839 [*NDJ*, 16 Jan 1865; drawings in NCRO (ZCR Maps 55)]

DISPENSARY, NELSON STREET, NEWCASTLE UPON TYNE, classical, 1839 [*NDJ*, 16 Jan 1865]

GAOL, CARLIOL SQUARE, NEWCASTLE UPON TYNE, minor additions, 1839 [*NC*, 24 May 1939]

TYNEMOUTH, TYNE AND WEAR (N), crescent and villas, for Messrs. Dawson and Bowes, 1839 [*NA*, 2 Feb, 1 June 1839]

WILLIAM CLARK MONUMENT, ST. AIDAN'S, BAMBURGH, NORTHUMBERLAND, Gothic, 1839 [*Durham Chronicle*, 21 Sep 1839]

ASYLUM FOR THE BLIND, NORTHUMBERLAND STREET, NEWCASTLE UPON TYNE, classical, 1840, dem. [*NDJ*, 16 Jan 1865]

CARLISLE, CUMBRIA, house for H. Bendle, 1840 [*NDJ*, 16 Jan 1865]

CHAPEL, ELSWICK, NEWCASTLE UPON TYNE, classical, unbuilt design, 1840 [ICBS No. 2421; drawings in Library, University of Newcastle upon Tyne]

EAST BOLDON HOUSE, TYNE AND WEAR (D), minor alterations for William Gray, 1840 [*NDJ*, 16 Jan 1865]

117

GATESHEAD, TYNE AND WEAR (D), viaduct for Brandling Junction Railway Co., 1840 [*NDJ*, 16 Jan 1865]

LINETHWAITE, BEDALE, CUMBRIA, house for H. Harrison, 1840 [*NDJ*, 16 Jan 1865]

MOOR HOUSE, RAINTON, COUNTY DURHAM, classical house for George Roper (?), 1840, dem. [Dobson, p89]

ST. PAUL'S, JARROW, TYNE AND WEAR (D), restoration, 1840 [Dobson, p106]

SWINBURNE CASTLE, NORTHUMBERLAND, restoration (?) for Thomas Riddell, 1840 [Dobson, p89]

ELSWICK, NEWCASTLE UPON TYNE, staithe for Elswick Lead Works, c.1840 [*NDJ*, 16 Jan 1865]

JESMOND HIGH TERRACE, NEWCASTLE UPON TYNE, classical terrace, c.1840, dem. 1960s [Dobson, p124]

LITTLE HARLE TOWER, NORTHUMBERLAND, unexecuted designs for classical additions to earlier house for Thomas Anderson, c.1840 [drawings in NCRO (NCRO 660/18)]

ST. MARY'S TERRACE, NEWCASTLE UPON TYNE, c.1840 [Dobson, p124]

ST. THOMAS'S PLACE, NEWCASTLE UPON TYNE, classical terrace, c.1840, dem. 1960s [*NDJ*, 16 Jan 1865]

BATHS, TERRACE AND HOTEL, ROKER TERRACE, MONKWEARMOUTH, TYNE AND WEAR (D), classical, 1840—1 [*NC*, 17 Apr 1840]

ST. PETER'S, OXFORD STREET, NEWCASTLE UPON TYNE, Gothic, 1840—3, dem. c.1936 [*NC*, 11 Mar 1842; ground plan in ICBS (2459)]

JESMOND ROAD, NEWCASTLE UPON TYNE, houses, including Carlton Terrace (Nos. 29—49) for 'Mr. Grey and Mr. Maughan' and others, c.1840—5; some dem. [*NC*, 16 Aug 1839; *NCh*, 7 Aug 1841; *NDJ*, 16 Jan 1865]

BROAD CHARE, NEWCASTLE UPON TYNE, warehouses for Trinity House, 1841 [*NC*, 26 Mar 1841]

CHEESEBURN GRANGE, NORTHUMBERLAND, addition of chapel (RC) for Ralph Riddell, 1841; rebuilt by Hansom [Dobson, p106]

RAILWAY STATION, LONDON ROAD, CARLISLE, CUMBRIA, Tudor, for the Newcastle and Carlisle Railway, 1841, dem. [Dobson, p118]

ST. OSWALD'S, ARNCLIFFE, YORKSHIRE, alterations, 1841 [Dobson, p107]

ST. PATRICKS (RC), FELLING, TYNE AND WEAR (D), Gothic, 1841, rebuilt 1893—5 [*NCh*, 5 June 1841]

117 ST. THOMAS OF CANTERBURY (RC), LONGHORSLEY, NORTHUMBERLAND, Gothic, 1841 [Dobson, p106]

TRINITY HOUSE, BROAD CHARE, NEWCASTLE UPON TYNE, alterations, 1841 [*AA* (V), XIII, p180]

ANGERTON HALL, NORTHUMBERLAND, Tudor house for Ralph Atkinson, 1842 [*NJ*, 15 Jan 1842]

ST. NICHOLAS'S, WEST BOLDON, TYNE AND WEAR (D), restoration, 1842 [*NDJ*, 16 Jan 1865]

SS MARY AND JOSEPH (RC), BIRTLEY, TYNE AND WEAR (D), Gothic, 1842—3 [*NC*, 20 May 1842]

118

118 SS MARY AND JOSEPH'S PRESBYTERY AND SCHOOL, BIRTLEY, TYNE AND WEAR (D), Tudor, 1842—3, school largely dem. [*NC*, 20 May 1842]

119 COLLINGWOOD MONUMENT, TYNEMOUTH, TYNE AND WEAR (N), classical, 1842—9, statue by Lough [*NC*, 28 Jan 1842]

BAMBURGH CASTLE, NORTHUMBERLAND, restoration for Lord Crewe's Trustees, 1843 [Dobson, p90]

119

BIRTLEY HALL, TYNE AND WEAR (D), house for
J. Warwick, 1843, dem. [*NDJ*, 16 Jan 1865]

CHAPEL, MINSTERACRES, NORTHUMBERLAND, for
George Silvertop, 1843 [Dobson, p107]

THE HAGS, HEXHAM, NORTHUMBERLAND, Tudor
house for Charles Head, 1843 [*NDJ*, 16 Jan 1865]

HARTBURN VICARAGE, NORTHUMBERLAND,
alterations for J. Hodgson, 1843 [Dobson, p115]

HIGH LEVEL BRIDGE, NEWCASTLE UPON TYNE,
unexecuted proposal, 1843 [*NC*, 22 Dec 1843]

REED MONUMENT, JESMOND CEMETERY,
NEWCASTLE UPON TYNE, Gothic, 1843 [*NC*, 23 Jun 1837]

ST. MARY'S, MORPETH, NORTHUMBERLAND,
restoration of nave, 1843 [*NDJ*, 16 Jan 1865]

LILBURN TOWER, NORTHUMBERLAND, alterations to
Dobson's 1828 house, for E.J. Collingwood 1843—4

SANDHOE HOUSE, HEXHAM, NORTHUMBERLAND,
Tudor house for Sir R.S. Errington, Bt., 1843—5 [*NC*, 14 Feb
1845; *NDJ*, 16 Jan 1865]

120 ST. ANDREW'S, NEWCASTLE UPON TYNE, addition of
south transept, neo-Norman, 1844 [*NDJ*, 16 Jan 1865]

120

WYNYARD PARK, CLEVELAND (D), arbitration with
Salvin and Donaldson in dispute between I. Bonomi and Lord
Londonderry, 1844

HAUGHTON CASTLE, NORTHUMBERLAND,
restorations for William Smith, 1844—5, further restorations
and additions by Salvin 1876 [*NDJ*, 16 Jan 1865; *History of
Northumberland*, XV, 1940, p214]

TOWN HALL, NORTH SHIELDS, TYNE AND WEAR (N),
originally included police offices, museum, bank and
Mechanics' Institution, Tudor, 1844—5 [*NC*, 28 Mar 1845]

BANK HOUSE, NEWBIGGIN, MIDDLETON-IN-
TEESDALE, COUNTY DURHAM, for John Hodgson
Hinde, 1845 [Dobson, p92]

CHATTON VICARAGE, NORTHUMBERLAND,
incorporating a pele tower, for Rev. Matthew Burrell, 1845
[*NC*, 10 Jan 1845; drawings NCRO (1875/C)]

CLEADON COTTAGE, TYNE AND WEAR (D), classical
house for Robert Swinburne, 1845, dem. 1981 [Dobson, p91]

THE KNELLS, CARLISLE, CUMBRIA, alterations (?) to
classical house for John Dixon, 1845 [*NDJ*, 16 Jan 1865]

CULLERCOATS, TYNE AND WEAR (N), rebuilding of
breakwater, 1846 [*NC*, 27 Nov 1846]

ST. STEPHEN'S, SOUTH SHIELDS, TYNE AND WEAR (D),
Gothic, 1846, dem. [*NDJ*, 16 Jan 1865]

SETTRINGTON VICARAGE, YORKSHIRE, 1846 [*NDJ*, 16
Jan 1865]

TRINITY PRESBYTERIAN CHURCH, NEW BRIDGE
STREET, NEWCASTLE UPON TYNE, Gothic, 1846—7,
dem. [*NC*, 21 Aug 1846]

121

121 ST. CUTHBERT'S, BENSHAM, TYNE AND WEAR (D),
neo-Norman, 1845—8, north aisle added 1875 [*NC*, 28 Mar
1845; plans and specifications in Society of Antiquaries,
London]

ALL SAINTS', FULWELL ROAD, MONKWEARMOUTH,
TYNE AND WEAR (D), Gothic, 1846—9 [*NC*, 3 Jly 1846]

CASTLE KEEP, NEWCASTLE, restoration, 1847 [*NDJ*,
16 Jan 1865]

CHOLLERTON VICARAGE, NORTHUMBERLAND,
additions, 1847 [drawings NCRO (1875/C)]

RIDING SCHOOL, NEWCASTLE UPON TYNE, classical,
1847 [*NDJ*, 16 Jan 1865]

122 BAPTIST CHAPEL, HOWARD STREET, NORTH
SHIELDS, TYNE AND WEAR (N), neo-Norman, 1846 [*NDJ*,
16 Jan 1865]

122

ST. AUGUSTINE'S, ALSTON, CUMBRIA, restoration, 1847,
rebuilt 1869—70 [Dobson, p109]

SS MARY AND THOMAS AQUINAS (RC), STELLA, TYNE
AND WEAR (D), additions, Gothic, 1847 [*NDJ*, 16 Jan 1865]

FLAX MILL, NEWCASTLE UPON TYNE, for R. Plummer,
1847—8 [*NC*, 6 Jan 1849]

CENTRAL RAILWAY STATION, NEWCASTLE UPON TYNE, classical, for York, Newcastle and Berwick Railway Co., and Newcastle and Carlisle Railway Co., 1847—50, portico added 1861—3 [*NC*, 15 Jan 1847; drawings in Laing Art Gallery and British Rail (Eastern)]

NORTH SHIELDS, TYNE AND WEAR (N), warehouse for North Shields and Tynemouth Railway, 1848 [*NCh*, 16 May 1848]

QUAYSIDE, NEWCASTLE UPON TYNE, proposed new quay, Customs House, warehouses, etc., 1848 [*NC*, 28 July 1848]

ST. ANDREW'S, WINSTON, COUNTY DURHAM, restoration, 1848 [*NDJ*, 16 Jan 1865]

ST. JOHN'S, NEWCASTLE UPON TYNE, restoration, 1848 [*NC*, 2 Jly 1847]

ST. MARY'S, STAMFORDHAM, NORTHUMBERLAND, restoration and additions, probably in conjunction with B. Ferrey, 1848 [*NC*, 21 April 1848; ICBS (No. 3971)]

WELTON, NORTHUMBERLAND, Tudor Keeper's Cottage and Directors' Rooms for Whittle Dean Water Company, 1848 [*NDJ*, 16 Jan 1865]

NORMAL SCHOOLS, SOUTH SHIELDS, TYNE AND WEAR (D), Tudor, for J. Stevenson, c.1848, dem. [*NDJ*, 16 Jan 1865]

PRESBYTERIAN CHURCH, FREDERICK STREET, SOUTH SHIELDS, TYNE AND WEAR (D), Gothic for J. Stevenson, 1848—9, dem. [*NJ*, 2 Sep 1848]

123 ST. CUTHBERT'S, SHOTLEY BRIDGE, COUNTY DURHAM, Gothic, 1848—50, additions made 1881—6 [*NC*, 1 Sep 1848; ground plan in ICBS (No. 3384)]

123

GATESHEAD, TYNE AND WEAR (D), main sewer, 1849 [Manders, p180; *AA* IV, 49, p153]

MANORS STATION AND GOODS WAREHOUSE, NEWCASTLE UPON TYNE, railway station etc., for York, Newcastle and Berwick Railway Co., 1849, dem. [*NC*, 27 Apr 1849]

STATION HOUSE, GATESHEAD, TYNE AND WEAR (D), railway station for York, Newcastle and Berwick Railway Co., 1849, dem. [*NC*, 27 Apr 1849]

ST. JOHN THE BAPTIST'S, MELDON, NORTHUMBERLAND, restoration, 1849 [*NDJ*, 16 Jan 1865]

ST. MICHAEL'S, BISHOPWEARMOUTH, TYNE AND WEAR (D), Gothic, addition of transepts, 1849—50 [*NCh*, 6 Jly 1849; ground plan in ICBS (No. 4148)]

HOLY TRINITY, EMBLETON, NORTHUMBERLAND, restoration 1850, chancel added 1866—7 [*NDJ*, 16 Jan 1865]

ELLISON MONUMENT, DONCASTER PARISH CHURCH, YORKS., for R. Ellison, c.1850, apparently destroyed with church in fire of 1853 [NDJ, 16 Jan 1865]

SCHOOLS, LYMM, CHESHIRE, 1850 [Dobson, p111]

STOCKTON-ON-TEES, VICARAGE, CLEVELAND (D), 1850 [*NDJ*, 16 Jan 1865]

WELTON, NORTHUMBERLAND, reservoir for Whittle Dene Water Company, 1850 [R.W. Rennison, *Water to Tyneside*, 1979, pp57—61]

BYWELL, NOTHUMBERLAND, cottages and schools for W.R. Beaumont, c.1850 [*NDJ*, 16 Jan 1865]

GRESHAM PLACE, NEWCASTLE UPON TYNE, classical villa for James Morrison, c.1850, dem. [*NC*, 29 May 1857]

TYNEMOUTH, TYNE AND WEAR (N), Priors Terrace, including house for Mr. Lawton, c.1850 [*NDJ*, 16 Jan 1865]

BARBER-SURGEONS' HALL, VICTORIA STREET, NEWCASTLE UPON TYNE, Italianate, 1850—1 [*NC*, 4 Oct 1850]

LYMM PARISH CHURCH, CHESHIRE, rebuilding, 1850—1 [*The Builder*, IX, 1851, p631]

124 BENFIELDSIDE VICARAGE, COUNTY DURHAM, Tudor, 1851 [*NJ*, 11 Jan 1851]

124

BRICKLAYERS' HALL, CASTLE GARTH, NEWCASTLE UPON TYNE, Gothic, 1851, dem. [*NJ*, 22 Nov 1851]

CHURCH HOUSE, WINDSOR, BERKSHIRE, for Rev. Dr. Stephen Hawtrey, 1851 [*NDJ*, 16 Jan 1865]

DENE HOUSE, JESMOND, NEWCASTLE UPON TYNE, Dobson's house of 1818 rebuilt for W. Cruddas, 1851, rebuilt by R.N. Shaw, 1870—85, additions by F.W. Rich, 1896—7 [Dobson, p94]

MANBY HOUSE, WARRINGTON, LANCASHIRE, additions, 1851 [Dobson, p92]

NEWTON HALL, BYWELL, NORTHUMBERLAND, alterations to 18th century house for W.H. Blackett, 1851 [Dobson, p93]

OATLANDS HOUSE, WEYBRIDGE, SURREY, Tudor house for William Chapman Hewitson, 1851, dem. 1972 [*NDJ*, 16 Jan 1865]

PENNYTHORNE HOUSE, MIDDLESBROUGH, CLEVELAND, house for A. Topham, 1851 [*NDJ*, 16 Jan 1865]

RYTON, TYNE AND WEAR (N), additions to house for Robert Leadbitter, 1851 [*NDJ*, 16 Jan 1865]

ST. MARY'S ALMSHOUSES, SCHOOL AND CHAPEL, RYE HILL, NEWCASTLE UPON TYNE, Gothic, 1851 [*NCh*, 22 Aug 1851]

ST. MARY MAGDALENE, GILSLAND, CUMBRIA, Gothic, 1851; the site architect was Stewart of Carlisle [*NDJ*, 16 Jan 1865]

STATION HOTEL, NEVILLE STREET, NEWCASTLE UPON TYNE, classical, 1851 [*NC*, 11 Jly 1851]

SUDBROOKE HOLME, LINCOLNSHIRE, large Tudor additions for Col. Richard Ellison, 1851, dem. [*NDJ*, 16 Jan 1865; J.C. Loudon *Cottage, Farm and Village Architecture*, pp1175—6]

ST. PAUL'S, HENDON, SUNDERLAND, TYNE AND WEAR (D), Gothic, 1851—2, dem. [*NC*, 20 Jun 1851; ground plan in ICBS (No. 4342)]

MONKWEARMOUTH, TYNE AND WEAR (D), planning and design of 400 houses in Dock Street, Ann Street, Dame Dorothy Street, Barrington Street, Harwicke Street, Bloomfield Street, Mulgrave Street, Normanby Street and Milburn Place, for Sir Hedworth Williamson, 1851—7, dem. [Fordyce, II, p480]

COLLEGE OF MEDICINE, ORCHARD STREET, NEWCASTLE UPON TYNE, Tudor, 1852, dem. c.1889 [*NC*, 14 May 1852]

DILDAWN HOUSE, KIRKCUDBRIGHTSHIRE, house for Rev. Dr. Cowan, 1852 [*NDJ*, 16 Jan 1865]

FRIEDELHAUSEN, W. GERMANY, largely unexecuted designs for Gothic castle for Adalbeit Baron von Nordeck zur Rabenau, 1852 [correspondence in Hessisches Staatsarchiv Marburg, Acc 1972/38, V, 9]

JOHN KNOX PRESBYTERIAN CHURCH, CLAYTON STREET WEST, NEWCASTLE UPON TYNE, Gothic, 1852, dem. c.1896 [*NC*, 24 Sep 1852]

125 PERCY CHAPEL, TYNEMOUTH PRIORY, TYNE AND WEAR (N), restoration, 1852 [*NCh*, 27 Aug 1852]

125

ST. PAUL'S RECTORY, HENDON, SUNDERLAND, TYNE AND WEAR (D), 1852, dem. [*NDJ*, 16 Jan 1865]

WESTMORELAND HOUSE, NEVILLE STREET, NEWCASTLE UPON TYNE, restoration in conjunction with building of Medical College, 1852, dem. [*NDJ*, 16 Jan 1865]

SEATON BURN, NORTHUMBERLAND, Tudor cottages, c.1852 [drawing in Private Collection]

ST. MICHAEL'S, FORD, NORTHUMBERLAND, restoration, 1852—3 [*NDJ*, 16 Jan 1865]

ST. STEPHEN'S NATIONAL SCHOOL, MILE END ROAD, SOUTH SHIELDS, TYNE AND WEAR (D), 1852—3; dem. [*NC*, 27 Aug 1852]

THE INFIRMARY, THE FORTH, NEWCASTLE UPON TYNE, alterations and new wing, 1852—5; dem. 1954 [Hume, G.H., *History of The Newcastle Infirmary*, 1906 pp51—60; lithographed plan in NCRO (309/N2/25/79)]

CLEADON MEADOWS, TYNE AND WEAR (D), house for Robert (or Richard) Shortridge, 1853, dem. [*NDJ*, 16 Jan 1865]

DIVINE UNITY CHURCH, NEW BRIDGE STREET, NEWCASTLE UPON TYNE, Gothic, 1853, dem. [*NC*, 22 Apr 1853]

DOCKS, NEWCASTLE UPON TYNE, proposals made by Dobson and W. Brooks, 1853 [*NCh*, 2 Dec 1853]

HOLY CROSS, CHATTON, NORTHUMBERLAND, restoration, 1853 [*NDJ*, 16 Jan 1865]

THE LEAZES, HEXHAM, NORTHUMBERLAND, Tudor additions, etc., to house for William Kirsopp, 1853 [Dobson, p95]

MUSEUM AND LIBRARY, WARRINGTON, CHESHIRE, classical, 1853; simplified version built, 1855—6 [Minutes of Warrington Council, 1853—4; drawings in Museum and Library, Warrington]

ST. MICHAEL'S RECTORY, BISHOPWEARMOUTH, TYNE AND WEAR (D), alterations to 18th century house, 1853 [*NDJ*, 16 Jan 1865]

SCHOOL, WHIXLEY, YORKSHIRE, 1853 [Dobson, p116]

WALLINGTON HALL, NORTHUMBERLAND, central hall, in courtyard of 17th and 18th century house, for Sir Walter Trevelyan, 1853—4 [*NDJ*, 16 Jan 1865; correspondence in Trevelyan Papers, Newcastle University]

ARCHBOLD MONUMENT, ST. NICHOLAS'S, NEWCASTLE UPON TYNE, classical, 1854 [*NC*, 21 Jly 1854]

RAGGED AND INDUSTRIAL SCHOOL, NEW ROAD, NEWCASTLE UPON TYNE, 1854, dem. [*NC*, 10 Mar 1854]

RECTORY PARK SCHOOLS, BISHOPWEARMOUTH, TYNE AND WEAR (D), Tudor, 1854, dem. [*NC*, 14 Jly 1854]

ROYAL JUBILEE SCHOOL, CITY ROAD, NEWCASTLE UPON TYNE, 'considerable alterations', to Dobson's 1810 building, 1854 [*NCh*, 29 Dec 1854]

WEST VIEW CEMETERY, HARTLEPOOL, CLEVELAND (D), chapels and entrance, 1854—5, dem. [*NC*, 30 Jun 1854]

ST. MARY'S, GATESHEAD, TYNE AND WEAR (D), restoration after Quayside fire, 1854—5 [*NC*, 27 Oct 1854]

QUAYSIDE, NEWCASTLE UPON TYNE, plans for rebuilding after fire, 1854—6 [*NC*, 27 Oct 1854; *NC*, 4 Jly 1856; perspective in Laing Art Gallery]

CASTLE KEEP, NEWCASTLE UPON TYNE, proposed conversion of Great Hall for museum, 1855, not carried out [*Proc. Soc. Ant.*, I, 1856, p81]

ST. CUTHBERT'S SCHOOL, BENSHAM, TYNE AND WEAR (D), 1855, dem. [*NC*, 5 Jan 1855]

ST. JOHN'S, NEWCASTLE UPON TYNE, refitting of chancel, 1855 [*NJ*, 27 Oct 1855]

SCAR HOUSE, ARKENDALE, W.R. YORKS., house for J. Gilpin, 1855 [*NDJ*, 16 Jan 1865]

SEGHILL VICARAGE, TYNE AND WEAR (N), Tudor, 1855 [*NC*, 20 Jly 1855]

ST. JOHN'S, OTTERBURN, NORTHUMBERLAND, Gothic, for Mrs. Askew and Miss Davison, 1855—7 [*NCh*, 12 Oct 1855]

BLACK GATE, NEWCASTLE UPON TYNE, proposed conversion to museum, with new street frontage, Gothic, 1856, not carried out [*AA*, ns, IV, p153; watercolour in private collection]

GIBSIDE, TYNE AND WEAR (D), alterations to 17th century house for W. Hutt, M.P., 1856 [*NDJ*, 16 Jan 1865]

LIVERPOOL, warehouses, 1856 [Dobson, p126]

NATURAL HISTORY SOCIETY OF NORTHUMBERLAND, DURHAM AND NEWCASTLE UPON TYNE, internal alterations, designed 1856, carried out by Thomas Austin, 1860 [T.R. Goddard, *History of The Natural History Society ...*, 1929, pp65-7]

ST. NICHOLAS'S, CRAMLINGTON,
NORTHUMBERLAND, proposed Gothic design, 1856, built
in altered and enlarged form by Austin & Johnson, 1865—8
[*NDJ*, 16 Jan 1865]

ST. COLUMBA'S PRESBYTERIAN CHURCH,
NORTHUMBERLAND SQUARE, NORTH SHIELDS,
TYNE AND WEAR (N), Italianate, 1856—7 [*NC*, 22 Aug
1856]

126 WESLEYAN CHAPEL, HOWARD STREET, NORTH
SHIELDS, TYNE AND WEAR (N), Italianate, 1856—7
[Latimer, p381, but also attributed to J. & B. Green]

SUNDERLAND, TYNE AND WEAR (D), South Dock grain
warehouse for George Hudson, 1856—8 [*NC*, 13 Jun 1856]

CHATTON, NORTHUMBERLAND, bridges, 1857 [*NC*,
23 Jan 1857]

INGLETHORPE HALL, EMNETH, NORFOLK, Tudor
Gothic house for Charles Metcalfe, 1857 [*The Builder*, XVIII,
1860, p12]

STATION HOTEL, LEEDS, YORKSHIRE, 1857 [Dobson,
p118]

WHITBY, YORKSHIRE, hotel, terrace and crescent,
including East Terrace, and Royal Crescent, for George
Hudson, 1857 [*NC*, 31 Jly 1857; site plan in Whitby Lit. &
Phil.]

ST PAUL'S, ELSWICK, NEWCASTLE UPON TYNE, Gothic,
1857—9 [*NC*, 27 Nov 1857; ground plans in ICBS (No. 5050)
and TWA (No. 530)]

LAMBTON CASTLE, COUNTY DURHAM, major
structural repairs and rebuilding of I. Bonomi's early 19th
century house, for the 2nd Earl of Durham, 1857—62,
completed by Sydney Smirke, 1862—6, and later partly dem.
[*NC*, 9 Oct 1857; drawing in Laing Art Gallery]

126

HOLEYN HALL, WYLAM, NORTHUMBERLAND, large
additions for Edward James, 1858 [*NDJ*, 16 Jan 1865]

HYLTON CASTLE, TYNE AND WEAR (D), survey for
repairs, etc., for John Bowes, 1858 [DCRO (Gibside Estate
Memo Book)]

NEWCASTLE COURANT OFFICE, GEORGE YARD,
NEWCASTLE UPON TYNE, 1858, dem. [*NC*, 12 Feb 1858]

RAGGED AND INDUSTRIAL SCHOOL, NEW ROAD,
NEWCASTLE UPON TYNE, additions, 1858, dem. [*NC*,
10 Sep 1858]

ST. MICHAEL'S RECTORY, BISHOPWEARMOUTH,
TYNE AND WEAR (D), installation of antique staircase, 1858
[*The Builder*, XVI, 1858, p319]

SHAWDON HALL, NORTHUMBERLAND, alterations for
John Pawson, 1858 [*NDJ*, 16 Jan 1865]

ST. MICHAEL'S, HOUGHTON-LE-SPRING, COUNTY
DURHAM, restoration, 1858—9 [*NC*, 12 Feb 1858]

THE PRIORY CHURCH OF ST. ANDREW, HEXHAM,
NORTHUMBERLAND, restoration of choir and east end,
partly in conjunction with A. Salvin, 1858—60 [Dobson, p100;
ground plan in ICBS (No. 5266)]

FREEMASONS' LODGE, MIDDLESBROUGH,
CLEVELAND, classical, 1858—61. dem. [*The Builder*, XIX,
1861, p84]

JESMOND PARISH CURCH, NEWCASTLE UPON TYNE,
Gothic, 1858—61 [*NJ*, 9 Apr 1859]

LITERARY AND PHILOSOPHICAL SOCIETY,
NEWCASTLE UPON TYNE, addition of lecture theatre, 1859
[*The Builder*, XVII, 1859, p275]

127 ST. NICHOLAS'S, NEWCASTLE UPON TYNE, rebuilding
of east end, 1859 [*AA*, ns, iv, pp152—3]

ST. JOHN'S, NEWCASTLE UPON TYNE, restoration, 1859
[Dobson, p104]

SCHOOL, BRANDON, COUNTY DURHAM, 1859 [*NC*,
12 Aug 1859]

OFFICE AND WORKERS' COTTAGES,
NORTHUMBERLAND DOCK, NORTH SHIELDS, TYNE
AND WEAR (N), classical, for Tyne Improvement
Commissioners, 1859—61, cottages dem. [*NC*, 27 May 1859]

JOHN KNOX PRESBYTERIAN CHURCH, CLAYTON
STREET WEST, NEWCASTLE UPON TYNE, addition of
galleries, 1860 [*NC*, 18 May 1860]

127.

'MAGDALEN GARDENS', proposed street to continue St.
Mary's Place, Newcastle upon Tyne, 1860, not carried out
[*NC*, 13 Jly 1860]

ST. GREGORY, KIRKNEWTON, NORTHUMBERLAND,
restoration and rebuilding, 1860 [*NJ*, 22 Apr 1860; ground plan
in ICBS (No. 5529)]

ST. LAURENCE'S, WARKWORTH,
NORTHUMBERLAND, restoration of nave, 1860 [*NJ*, 20 Oct
1860]

ST. PETER'S, OXFORD STREET, NEWCASTLE UPON
TYNE, completion of tower and spire, Gothic, 1860, dem.,
c.1936 [*NC*, 16 Mar 1860]

SEATON DELAVAL, NORTHUMBERLAND, repairs after
fire for Sir Astley, Bt., 1860 [Dobson, p26]

TYNEMOUTH, TYNE AND WEAR (N), proposed crescents,
etc., at Tynemouth Lodge for William Linskill, 1860
[prospectus in NCRO (ZMD 68/7)]

UNTHANK HALL, NORTHUMBERLAND, additions for
Dixon Dixon, 1860 [Dobson, p75]

JESMOND DENE, NEWCASTLE UPON TYNE, additions,
including separate Italianate Banqueting House, for Sir
William Armstrong, 1860—2, dem. 1920s [Dobson, p96]

ST. EDWARD'S, SUDBROOKE, LINCS., neo-Norman, for R. Ellison, 1860—2 [*NDJ*, 16 Jan 1865]

GAOL, CARLIOL SQUARE, NEWCASTLE UPON TYNE, major additions, 1861, dem. [*NC*, 8 Feb 1861; drawings in TWA (782)]

GREENWOOD, EASTLEIGH, HAMPSHIRE, house for George Palmer, 1861, dem. [*NDJ*, 16 Jan 1865]

ST. MARY'S, COWPEN, Nr. BLYTH, NORTHUMBERLAND, Gothic, 1861, completed in modified form by Austin & Johnson, 1864 [*NC*, 20 Dec 1861]

GAS COMPANY OFFICE, NEVILLE STREET, NEWCASTLE UPON TYNE, Italianate, 1861—2, dem. c.1971 [*NDJ*, 16 Jan 1865; drawing in TWA (1193)]

ST. MARY'S, TYNE DOCK, SOUTH SHIELDS, TYNE AND WEAR (D), Gothic, 1861—2 dem. 1982 [*NC*, 8 Feb 1861]

CENTRAL STATION, NEWCASTLE UPON TYNE, addition of portico, 1861, executant architect Thomas Prosser [drawings with British Rail (Eastern)]

MECHANICS' INSTITUTE, ELSWICK, NEWCASTLE UPON TYNE, for Sir William Armstrong, 1862 [*NC*, 2 Sep 1862]

ST. NICHOLAS'S, NEWCASTLE UPON TYNE, proposed restoration of steeple, 1862, not carried out [*AA*, fourth series, IX, p145]

CASTLETON HOUSE, SUNDERLAND, TYNE AND WEAR (D), house for Mr. Mounsey [*NDJ*, 16 Jan 1865]

CHESTER, CHESHIRE, house [*NDJ*, 16 Jan 1865]

EBCHESTER, COUNTY DURHAM, house for M.R. Bigge [*NDJ*, 16 Jan 1865]

EGLINGHAM PARISH CHURCH, NORTHUMBERLAND, restoration [*NDJ*, 16 Jan 1865]

HIGH CROSS HOUSE, BENWELL, NEWCASTLE UPON TYNE, house for Mr. Buddle [*NDJ*, 16 Jan 1865]

HOLY ISLAND, NORTHUMBERLAND, beacons [Dobson, p121]

HYLTON LODGE, CHIRTON, TYNE AND WEAR (N), house for Thomas Hughes, dem. [*NDJ*, 16 Jan 1865]

MILBURN HALL, NORTHUMBERLAND, bridge [*NDJ*, 16 Jan 1865]

NETHERWITTON VICARAGE, NORTHUMBERLAND [*NDJ*, 16 Jan 1865]

NORTH MIDDLEHAM RECTORY, YORKSHIRE, for M. Birch [*NDJ*, 16 Jan 1865]

NORTH SHIELDS, TYNE AND WEAR (N), plans and sections for North Shields and Tynemouth Railway [*NDJ*, 16 Jan 1865]

PONTELAND VICARAGE, NORTHUMBERLAND [*NDJ*, 16 Jan 1865]

REFORMATORY, NETHERTON, NORTHUMBERLAND [Dobson, p130]

ST. BRANDON'S, BRANCEPETH, COUNTY DURHAM, restoration [*NDJ*, 16 Jan 1865]

SOUTH SHIELDS, TYNE AND WEAR (D), new quay [Dobson, p127]

TEMPERLEY GRANGE, CORBRIDGE, NORTHUMBERLAND, alterations for Mr. Hopper [*NDJ*, 16 Jan 1865]

WYNYARD PARK, CLEVELAND (D), 'alterations' [*NDJ*, 16 Jan 1865]